COLLEGE MAJORS

Second Edition

COLLEGE MAJORS

A Complete Guide from Accounting to Zoology

Second Edition

Ellen Lederman

McFarland & Company, Inc., Publishers
Jefferson, North Carolina, and London

LIBRARY OF CONGRESS CATALOGUING-IN-PUBLICATION DATA

Lederman, Ellen, 1954–
    College majors : a complete guide from accounting to
zoology / Ellen Lederman.— 2nd ed.
        p.   cm.

    ISBN-13: 978-0-7864-2888-5
    (softcover : 50# alkaline paper) ∞

    1. Degrees, Academic — United States — Directories.
2. Universities and colleges — Curricula — United States —
Directories.   I. Title.
LB2390.L43   2007
378.1'9902573 — dc22   2006032218

British Library cataloguing data are available

On the cover: guitar strings and vegetable garden
©2006 PhotoSpin; medical lab ©2006 Corbis Images

Manufactured in the United States of America

McFarland & Company, Inc., Publishers
    Box 611, Jefferson, North Carolina 28640
    www.mcfarlandpub.com

Table of Contents

Table of Contents

Table of Contents

Table of Contents

Preface

Whether you are planning for college or are currently enrolled, you will still be required at some point (usually by the end of your sophomore year) to declare a major. If you are like most students, you will find that choosing a major field of study is not an easy task. It requires a great deal of introspection, forcing you to think about the person you are right now and the person you would like to become. You need to define your personal strengths and weaknesses, interests, and goals. Your next step is to find a major that best suits your needs. Since there are over 400 possible college majors, it can be difficult to zero in on the one major that is right for you.

College Majors: A Complete Guide from Accounting to Zoology provides a starting point for making this crucial decision. It will not tell you every possible detail about each major, but it will enable you to screen out those majors that are of no interest while discovering a few majors that are worthy of further consideration. Once you find three to five possibilities, you can explore each in greater detail. Speak with professors and students in your tentative field to learn more about the major. Study college catalogs to learn about the requirements and curriculums. Utilize resources such as career books, *The Guide for Occupational Exploration, Occupational Outlook Handbook,* and so on, available online, in libraries, and from book sellers.

In addition to choosing a program of study, you will also need to choose a specific college or university. Your college choice will be affected by such factors as location and expenses, as well as personal preferences and admissions requirements. The scope of this book does not permit a listing of the schools that offer each particular major. After you have finalized your choice of major, you can research individual college catalogs or the major comprehensive guides

1

to colleges. This will help you pinpoint which colleges offer which majors.

Many students change their college majors at least once during their college careers. To some extent, this is to be expected since people change and grow. The interests and ambitions with which they started college may be entirely different a year or two later. Changing a college major should not necessarily be construed as a negative occurrence, but it can be costly in terms of time and money. It can require an extra year or two in college. It may even necessitate transferring to a different school. If you are having difficulty finalizing your choice of major, try to attend a school that offers a few majors that you find interesting. Most importantly, spend sufficient time learning about the majors and about yourself. Work at making the best possible decision so that your decision can work for you in all the years to come.

Introduction

College Majors: A Complete Guide from Accounting to Zoology provides descriptions of all majors offered at the college level. Only those majors in which an associate, baccalaureate, master's, or doctoral level degree can be obtained are included. While some colleges offer limited coursework or certificate programs in additional areas, these courses are not mentioned here if they do not constitute a major area leading to a degree.

The information in this book was compiled from hundreds of college catalogs. Although no two colleges or universities offer identical programs, it was possible to analyze general trends. Common elements of the various major coursework were discovered. The author's background in vocational evaluation and career counseling was helpful in delineating the needed abilities and career possibilities.

Although *College Majors* is largely self-explanatory, the following information may further clarify the descriptions of these majors.

Level(s) offered

Associate Degree

The two types of associate degree programs are:

(1) technological and vocational specialties (such as carpentry or occupational therapy assisting), leading to direct entrance into an occupational field.

(2) college- or university parallel programs (such as French or biology) which simulate the first two years of a four-year college curriculum and allow direct transfer into a bachelor's program. Associate degree programs are offered at technical,

community, and junior colleges and typically require two years to complete.

Baccalaureate or Bachelor's Degree

This degree generally involves four years of full-time study, although a few (such as architecture) can require five years. Majors include the liberal arts, sciences, business, technology, and specific vocational programs. For most professions and occupations, this is the minimum entry-level degree.

Master's Degree

A master's degree program requires one to two years of full-time study beyond the bachelor's degree. Most majors at the bachelor's level are offered at the master's level, enabling the student to build upon his or her previous exposure to the field. It can also be possible to major in a different field and then pursue graduate schooling in a new major, especially if the undergraduate degree provided some preparation for the graduate program (such as an undergraduate degree in psychology enabling graduate study in counseling or social work). Some vocationally oriented majors require this degree for full professional status (e.g. social work, library science, health care administration).

Doctoral Degree

A doctoral degree usually requires at least three years of full-time equivalent academic work beyond the baccalaureate level. Doctoral programs allow for highly specialized, individualized study. Degrees at this advanced level are typically required for professional positions in the science and for teaching at the college level. Some undergraduate majors are not available as a doctoral degree program since there is not enough depth of these bodies of knowledge to warrant the extensive research and study demanded by this degree program.

No book can tell you which level of degree is best for you. Only you know your own circumstances. If your funds are limited, for example, you may want to initially earn an associate or bachelor's degree, start working, and eventually obtain a master's degree (especially if your employer has a tuition reimbursement program). If academic work has always been difficult for you, it may not be realistic to pursue a graduate degree.

Typical Courses

No two colleges offer exactly the same curriculum in a particular major. The types of courses available at each college reflect the faculty's expertise and interests. Some colleges offer narrowly circumscribed coursework, whereas others provide as many as fifty elective courses within a major. Keep in mind that the courses listed in this section are only a sampling of representative courses in the major. You will need to consult the catalogs of the colleges of your choice to discover exactly what courses are offered.

Related/Complementary Majors

This section is included because you may find yourself enrolled at a college that does not offer the major in question. For various reasons, you may not be able to attend a school that offers exactly the major you want. You may, however, be able to find a major that is closely related to your original choice. For example, you might opt to major in interior design, urban design, or architecture if an environmental design major is not available.

Another reason for this section is to show some possibilities for a double major (or a minor). A carefully chosen second major that complements the first can greatly expand your knowledge base and give you a competitive edge in the job market. Students who major in technical and business writing/communication, for instance, generally find many career opportunities within this field, but they will be even more desirable to potential employers if they have additional expertise in the area they'll be writing about (i.e. business, finance, computers, science). Each school has its own criteria for a dual major or minor, so be sure to check out the requirements before you make any decisions.

Needed Abilities

Different majors require different abilities. A student who has the aptitude for engineering may not be as successful in an education major.

When choosing your major, you need to be honest with yourself about your own abilities. While some of the abilities, aptitudes, and skills listed in this section can be developed or improved to some extent, your greatest chances for success are in those majors that demand abilities similar to your own.

Some of the most frequently needed abilities for individual majors include:

Analytical ability— The ability to discover the various components of a problem. This does not necessarily indicate the ability to solve the problem. For example, some pure scientific fields (such as pathology or microbiology), philosophy, or anthropology may investigate phenomena or analyze theories but may not attempt to make any changes or develop solutions.

Creativity— The ability to think of unique ways to perform a technique, solve a problem, or develop a new approach.

Interpersonal skills— The ability to relate well to other people.

Manual dexterity— The ability to use the hands to manipulate objects.

Orientation to details— The ability to focus on each individual aspect of a situation or object rather than looking at it in its entirety.

Physical strength and stamina— The ability to lift heavy objects and tolerate other physical demands such as frequent standing or walking.

Visual perception— The ability to perceive details of form and space of objects.

Career Possibilities

The major you choose will have a direct impact on your employment opportunities. While it is true that many people work in areas unrelated to their major, usually your degree will have a bearing on the first job you obtain and subsequent jobs thereafter. The career possibilities listed in this section alert you to only a few of the occupations typically performed by graduates in that major.

THE MAJORS

Accounting

Describes the principles, procedures, and theories of organizing, maintaining, and auditing business and financial transactions.

Levels offered: Associate, Bachelor's, Master's, Doctoral.

Typical courses: Federal Income Tax, Auditing, Accounting for Nonprofit Organizations, International Financial Accounting, Cost Accounting.

Related/complementary majors: Business Administration and Management, Taxation.

Needed abilities: excellent aptitude for mathematics, analytical ability, problem-solving skills, orientation for details.

Career possibilities: accountant, business manager.

Actuarial Sciences

Describes the mathematical and statistical methods dealing with problems of risks in insurance.

Levels offered: Bachelor's, Master's, Doctoral.

Typical courses: Numerical Analysis, Statistics, Probability, Advanced Calculus, Linear Algebra.

Related/complementary majors: Insurance and Risk Management, Mathematics, Statistics, Finance, Applied Mathematics.

Needed abilities: excellent aptitude for mathematics, analytical ability, problem-solving skills.

Career possibilities: insurance/business/financial services actuary.

Administrative Office Technology

Prepares individuals to perform a variety of clerical duties and assume some administrative functions to keep an office running smoothly.

Levels offered: Associate.

Typical courses: Advanced Word Processing Applications, Accounting Principles, Legal Environment of Business, Information Management, Database Management.

Related/complementary courses: Business Administration and Management.

Needed abilities: keyboarding and computer skills, attention to detail, aptitude for applied business, managerial skills.

Career possibilities: office manager/worker.

Adult Education

Describes the theories, methods, and techniques of designing and implementing instruction for adult learners.

Levels offered: Bachelor's, Master's, Doctoral.

Typical courses: Teaching the Disadvantaged Adult, Adult Education Practicum, Teaching in Nonschool Settings, Nature of Adult Education, Community Concepts and Programs.

Related/complementary majors: Adult and Continuing Education Administration, Human Resources Management/Personnel Administration.

Needed abilities: excellent interpersonal/communication skills.

Career possibilities: corporate trainer, teacher of Adult Basic Education, community college instructor, adult evening class instructor.

Advertising

Describes the creation, execution, transmission, and evaluation of commercial messages concerned with the promotion and sale of products and services.

Levels offered: Bachelor's, Master's, Doctoral (limited number of programs).

Typical courses: Theories of Advertising, Advertising Copy, Sales Promotion, Advertising Management, Advertising Research.

Related/complementary majors: Business Administration and Management, Communications, Graphic Illustration, Industrial Design, Marketing/Research, Public Relations.

Needed abilities: aptitude for visual or verbal expression, creativity, good interpersonal skills.

Career possibilities: advertising/sales worker (account executive, copywriter, sales representative, advertising director).

Aeronautics/Aeronautical Technology

Prepares individuals to assist engineers and other professionals in the design, testing, and development of propulsion, control, and guidance systems of aircraft and aerospace vehicles.

Levels offered: Associate, Bachelor's, Master's.

Typical courses: Aerospace Systems Design, Aircraft Design, Aircraft Accident Investigation, Combustion Analysis, Electro-mechanical Control Systems.

Related/complementary majors: Drafting, Engineering (Aerospace, Aeronautical, Astronautical, Mechanical), Aerospace Science.

Needed abilities: aptitude for applied physics and mathematics, analytical ability, problem-solving skills and creativity, orientation for details and precision, ability to deal with complex machinery and instrumentation.

Career possibilities: aeronautical maintenance technologist, aeronautical operations technician, small craft designer.

Aerospace/Aeronautical/ Astronautical Engineering

Describes the design, construction, operation, and maintenance of aircraft, space vehicles, and power units, and the special programs of flight in both the earth's atmosphere and space.

Levels offered: Bachelor's, Master's, Doctoral.

Typical courses: Atmospheric and Space Flight Mechanics, Environmental Aerodynamics, Gas Dynamics, Aeroelasticity, Computational Aerodynamics.

Related/complementary majors: Aeronautical Technology, Astrophysics, Atmospheric Sciences and Meteorology.

Needed abilities: excellent aptitude for physical science and mathematics, strong analytical ability, strong problem-solving skills.

Career possibilities: aerospace/aeronautical engineer, astronaut, test pilot.

Aerospace Science/Studies

Prepares for Air Force careers.

Levels offered: Bachelor's.

Typical courses: Air Force Today, Leadership Lab, Development of Air Power, National Security.

Related/complementary majors: Aerospace/Aeronautical/Astronautical Engineering, Military Science.

Needed abilities: ability to be commissioned into the Air Force and perform assigned technical and leadership duties.

Career possibilities: Air Force officer.

African Studies

Describes the history, society, politics, culture, and economics of Africa.

Levels offered: Bachelor's, Master's Doctoral.

Typical courses: History of West Africa, African Religions. African Music and Dance, African Political Systems. History of African Civilizations.

Related/complementary majors: African-American Studies, Anthropology, Art History, Economics, Geography, History, International Relations, Music History and Appreciation, Political Science and Government, Religion, Sociology.

Needed abilities: aptitude for social science, analytical ability, interest in and sensitivity to other cultures.

Career possibilities: diplomat, Peace Corps or missionary worker.

African-American/Black Studies

Describes the history, society, politics, culture, and economics of African-Americans.

Levels offered: Bachelor's, Master's, Doctoral.

Typical courses: African-American Art, The Black Novel, The Black Woman in America, Contemporary Black Film, Black Music in America.

Related/complementary majors: American Studies, Art Appreciation and History, Comparative Literature, Economics, History, Music History and Appreciation, Political Science, Religion, Sociology, Urban Studies.

Needed abilities: aptitude for social science, analytical ability.

Career possibilities: African-American affairs writer, worker/director of a program that focuses on African-Americans.

Agricultural Business and Management/Agri-Business

Prepares individuals to apply the economic and business principles involved in the organization, operation, and management of farm and agricultural business.

Levels offered: Associate, Bachelor's, Master's, Doctoral.

Typical courses: Farm Management, Farm Records, Soil and Water Management, Animal Husbandry.

Related/complementary majors: Agricultural Economics, International Agriculture.

Needed abilities: aptitude for business principles and practices, scientific aptitude for agricultural practices, analytical ability, problem-solving skills.

Career possibilities: agricultural manager, marketing representative for an agricultural business.

Agricultural Economics

Prepares individuals to apply economic principles relating to the allocation of resources in the production and marketing of agricultural products and services in the domestic and international markets.

Levels offered: Bachelor's, Master's, Doctoral.

Typical courses: Agricultural Prices, International Agricultural Analysis, Distribution and Marketing, of Agricultural Products, Agricultural Futures Trading.

Related/complementary majors: Agricultural Business and Management, Economics.

Needed abilities: excellent aptitude for business principles and mathematics, analytical ability.

Career possibilities: agricultural economist.

Agricultural and Extension Education

Prepares individuals to teach agriculture in formal and informal learning settings.

11

Levels offered: Bachelor's, Master's, Doctoral.

Typical courses: Problems in Agriculture and Extension Education, Agriculture Education Student Teaching, Planning Community College Programs in Adult Education, Facilitating Leadership in Adult Education, and Foundations and Philosophies of Teaching Adult Education.

Related/complementary majors: Science Education, Secondary Education.

Needed abilities: aptitude for biological and physical science, excellent communication skills.

Career possibilities: secondary or community college agricultural teacher, extension agent.

Agricultural Engineering

Describes the design, construction, operation, and maintenance of equipment, structures, machinery, and energy devices for producing food and fiber.

Levels offered: Bachelor's, Master's, Doctoral.

Typical courses: Advanced Farm Power and Machinery, Dynamics of Tillage and Traction, Agricultural Structures Design, Soil and Water Engineering, Biological and Physical Systems Analysis.

Related/complementary majors: Agricultural Technology.

Needed abilities: excellent aptitude for physical science, biology and mathematics, analytical ability, problem-solving skills.

Career possibilities: agricultural engineer.

Agricultural Mechanization/Technology

Describes the theoretical and technical knowledge needed to service agricultural equipment.

Levels offered: Associate.

Typical courses: Agricultural Technology Basic Hydraulics, Air Conditioning, Harvesting Equipment, Power Train Repair, Set Up and Delivery.

Related/complementary majors: Agricultural Engineering, Diesel Engine Mechanics.

Needed abilities: mechanical aptitude, understanding of agricultural science.

Career possibilities: agricultural equipment sales and service representative.

Agriculture, General

Provides a general overview of the principles and practices of agricultural research and production.

Levels offered: Associate, Bachelor's.

Typical courses: Introduction to Poultry Science, Principles of Weed Science, Marketing Agricultural Products, Farm Management, Sustainable Agriculture.

Related/complementary majors: any agricultural specialty major.

Needed abilities: aptitude for biological and physical science, as well as business.

Career possibilities: farm manager, agricultural production manager, sales representative for agricultural products.

Agronomy

Describes the principles and practices involved in the development, production, and management of field crops.

Levels offered: Associate, Bachelor's, Master's, Doctoral.

Typical courses: Biophysical Crop Ecology, Principles of Weed Science, Cytogenics in Plant Breeding, Soil Microbiology, Grain Crop Management.

Related/complementary majors: Botany, Plant Protection, Soil Sciences.

Needed abilities: strong aptitude for biological, chemical, and physical sciences, analytical ability, problem-solving skills.

Career possibilities: field agronomist, plant/food/grain inspector.

Air Conditioning, Refrigeration, and Heating Technology

Prepares individuals to design, install, maintain, and operate air conditioning, heating, and refrigeration systems.

Levels offered: Associate (very limited number of Bachelor's).

Typical courses: Commercial Refrigeration, Mechanical Codes, Duct Construction and Design, Theory of Refrigeration, Basic Electricity.

Related/complementary majors: Mechanical Engineering.

Needed abilities: aptitude for applied physics and technology, analytical ability, problem-solving skills, excellent mechanical ability.

Career possibilities: air conditioning/heating/refrigeration mechanic.

Aircraft Mechanics

Prepares individuals to repair, service, and overhaul all airplane parts.

Levels offered: Associate.

Typical courses: Airframe Shop, Airframe Theory, Powerplant Shop, Powerplant Maintenance, General Aircraft Maintenance.

Related/complementary majors: Aeronautical Technology.

Needed abilities: aptitude for applied physics, excellent mechanical ability, analytical ability, problem-solving skills.

Career possibilities: aircraft mechanic (airframe or power plant).

American Indian Studies/ Native American Studies

Describes the history, society, politics, and culture of Native Americans.

Levels offered: Associate, Bachelor's, Master's, Doctoral.

Typical courses: American Indian Military Campaigns, Native American Art Appreciation. Introduction to Indian Education, Historical and Sociocultural Examination of Indian America, native American Contributions in Science, Medicine, and Agriculture.

Related/complementary majors: Anthropology, Art History and Appreciation, History, Museum Studies, Music History and Appreciation, Political Science and Government, Sociology.

Needed abilities: aptitude for social science and appreciation for Native American history and culture.

Career possibilities: museum curator, worker/director of Indian Affairs programs.

American Studies

Describes the history, society, politics, culture, and economics of the United States.

Levels offered: Bachelor's, Master's, Doctoral.

Typical courses: Issues in American Civilization, Historical Perspectives on American Culture, Interpretations of American Culture, Literature of America.

Related/complementary majors: Economics, History, Political Science, Sociology.

Needed abilities: excellent aptitude for social science, analytical ability.

Career possibilities: teacher, writer.

Anatomy

Describes the structure of plants and animals, including their tissues, organs, and systems.

Levels offered: Master's, Doctoral.

Typical courses: Advanced Histology of Domestic Animals, Microscopic Anatomy, Cardiovascular Anatomy, Neuroanatomy.

Related/complementary majors: Medical Illustration, Pathology, Physiology, Zoology.

Needed abilities: excellent aptitude for biological science, ability to visualize and memorize complex structures.

Career possibilities: research scientist, teacher,

Animal Science

Describes the theories, principles, and applications of appropriate technical skills that apply to the production and management of animals and animal products.

Levels offered: Associate, Bachelor's, Master's, Doctoral.

Typical courses: Animal Health, Hygiene, and Parasitology, Dairy Cattle Genetics and Breeding, Behavior of Farm Animals, Applied Animal Nutrition, Animal Anatomy and Physiology.

Related/complementary majors: Dairy, Genetics, Pathology, Physiology, Poultry, Zoology.

Needed abilities: strong aptitude for biological science, ability to apply business principles to agricultural practices, analytical ability, problem-solving skills.

Career possibilities: animal breeder, animal technician, sales representative for animal nutrition and care company.

Anthropology

Describes the historic and prehistoric origins of man, including physical and cultural development, racial characteristics, social customs, and beliefs.

Levels offered: Associate, Bachelor's, Master's, Doctoral.

Typical courses: Problems in Ethnology, Physical Anthropology, Population Dynamics, Middle East Culture, Field Methods in Linguistics.

Related/complementary majors: Archaeology, specific area and ethnic studies, Sociology.

Needed abilities: aptitude for history and sociology, analytical ability.

Career possibilities: researcher, museum worker, employee of a federal agency that deals with cultural affairs.

Applied Behavioral Analysis

Describes the process of systematically applying interventions based on upon the principles of learning theory to improve socially significant behaviors (such as reading, academics, social skills, communication skills, and adaptive living skills) and to demonstrate that the interventions employed are responsible for the improvement of behavior.

Levels offered: Bachelor's, Master's.

Typical courses: Principles of Learning, Direct Observation Methods and Functional Assessment, Applied Behavior Analysis in Complex Community Settings, Building Skills with Behavior Technology, Behavior Principles and Self-Management.

Related/complementary majors: Psychology.

Needed abilities: aptitude for psychology, statistics, and data management; analytical ability, problem-solving skills.

Career possibilities: behavior analyst.

Applied Mathematics

Describes the real world systems by deterministic and probabilistic models.

Levels offered: Bachelor's, Master's, Doctoral.

Typical courses: Advanced Calculus, Differential Equations,

Numerical Analysis, Models in Applied Mathematics, Mathematical Statistics.

Related/complementary majors: Statistics.

Needed abilities: excellent mathematical aptitude, analytical ability, problem-solving skills.

Career possibilities: mathematician, teacher.

Archaeology

Describes the historic and prehistoric peoples and their cultures through the scientific analysis of the artifacts, inscriptions, monuments, and other remains.

Levels offered: Bachelor's, Master's, Doctoral.

Typical courses: Archaeology of Egypt, World Cultural Regions, Archaeological Resource Management, Analysis of Archaeological Data, Archaeology of Greek and Roman Statues.

Related/complementary majors: Anthropology, History, Museology.

Needed abilities: aptitude for history and anthropology, orientation to visual details, analytical ability.

Career possibilities: antiques dealer, archaeologist, museum curator.

Architectural Technology

Prepares individuals to support and assist architects in planning and designing structures and buildings; testing materials; constructing and inspecting structures; model building and design estimating; utilizing, transporting, and storing construction materials; and dealing with contacts and specifications.

Levels offered: Associate, Bachelor's.

Typical courses: Blueprint Reading for the Construction Industry, Design Development for Architectural Technicians, Specifications and Materials for Building Construction, Fundamentals of Drafting for Building Construction, Codes and Ordinances.

Related/complementary majors: Construction, Drafting and Design Technology.

Needed abilities: good aptitude for applied physics and mathematics, eye for visual details, analytical ability, problem-solving skills, ability to work under the direction of an architect.

17

Career possibilities: architectural technician, construction foreman.

Architecture

Describes the processes that promote the use of aesthetic patterns, forms, and structures for human purposes in harmony with the environment.

Levels offered: Bachelor's, Master's, Doctoral.

Typical courses: Computer-Aided Architectural and Environmental Design, Architectural Photography, Architectural Acoustic Environment, Human Habitat, History, Theory, and Criticism of Medieval Architecture.

Related/complementary majors: Environmental Design.

Needed abilities: eye for artistic detail, excellent visual (space and form) perception, analytical ability, problem-solving skills, creativity, aptitude for applied physics and mathematics.

Career possibilities: architect.

Archival Studies

Prepares individuals to collect, organize, and control information deemed important enough for permanent safekeeping, such as photographs, films, letters, documents, and so on.

Levels offered: Master's, Doctoral (limited number of programs).

Typical courses: Archives and Manuscripts, Preservation Management, Seminar in Archives and Records Management, Public History: Methods and Theory, Management of Electronic Records.

Related/complementary majors: Library and Information Science, History.

Needed abilities: ability to adhere to prescribed methods, analytical ability, problem-solving skills, appreciation of history.

Career possibilities: archivist.

Art Education

Describes the theories, methods, and techniques involved in teaching the subject matter of art.

Levels offered: Bachelor's, Master's, Doctoral.

Typical courses: Approaches for Public School Art, Teaching for

Art Appreciation, Art for Special Needs Children, Approaches for Art Curriculum and Supervision, Approaches for Art Curriculum and Supervision, Foundations for Teaching Visual arts.

Related/complementary majors: Education (elementary or secondary).

Needed abilities: excellent communication and interpersonal skills, creativity, artistic ability.

Career possibilities: art teacher.

Art History and Appreciation

Describes art and its relationship to current events, the evaluation of artistic styles, the lives of artists, and the role of art in human affairs, including contemporary times.

Levels offered: Associate, Bachelor's, Master's, Doctoral.

Typical courses: Greek and Roman Art, Early Renaissance Art, Modern Art, Art of the Eighteenth Century.

Related/complementary majors: Anthropology, specific area and ethnic studies, Fine Arts (drawing, painting, sculpture), History, Medieval and Renaissance Studies, Museum Studies, Religion.

Needed abilities: aptitude for history and social science, eye for visual detail, understanding of art processes, techniques, and styles, analytical ability.

Career possibilities: art educator, art journalist/writer, museum curator.

Art Therapy

Prepares individuals to apply the principles and techniques of art to the rehabilitation of physically or mentally ill patients.

Levels offered: Master's, Doctoral.

Typical courses: psychology of Art, Child Case Studies in Art Therapy, Psychodrama in Art Therapy, Projective Measures of Personality, Expressive Arts Therapy.

Related/complementary majors: Occupational Therapy, Psychology.

Needed abilities: aptitude for psychology and art, analytical ability, problem-solving skills, creativity, excellent interpersonal skills.

Career possibilities: art therapist.

Arts Management

Prepares individuals to apply business principles to the management and operation of profit and nonprofit organizations that specialize in the visual or performing arts.

Levels offered: Bachelor's, Master's.

Typical courses: Accounting for the Arts, Grant Proposal Planning and Writing, Computer Uses for the Business of the Arts, Marketing the Arts, Labor Relations for the Arts.

Related/complementary majors: Business Administration and Management, Crafts, Dance, Dramatic Arts, Film Arts, Fine Arts, Music.

Needed abilities: understanding of the arts, aptitude for business, analytical ability, problem-solving skills, good interpersonal skills.

Career possibilities: agent, business manager, producer, manager of program, facility, or organization in the arts.

Asian Studies

Describes the history, society, politics, and economics of Asia.

Levels offered: Bachelor's, Master's, Doctoral.

Typical courses: Music of Asia, Buddhist Studies, South Asian Civilization, Asia Through Fiction, Japanese Economics.

Related/complementary majors: Anthropology, Art History and Appreciation, Comparative Literature, Economics, History, International Business Management, International Relations, languages (such as Chinese, Japanese, Korean), Music History and Appreciation, Political Science, Religion.

Needed abilities: excellent aptitude for all areas of social sciences (economics, history, political science, sociology), analytical ability.

Career possibilities: businessperson with an international firm, diplomatic worker.

Astronomy

Describes matter and energy in the universe, including the solar system, stars, galaxies, and nebula.

Levels offered: Associate, Bachelor's, Master's, Doctoral.

Typical courses: Cosmology, Astronomical Spectroscopy, General Relativity, Stellar Atmospheres, Basic Properties of Galaxies.

Related/complementary majors: Astrophysics, Planetary Science.

Needed abilities: excellent aptitude for physical science, aptitude for mathematics, analytical ability.

Career possibilities: teacher, planetarium worker, astronomy researcher.

Astrophysics

Describes the physical and chemical composition of celestial bodies, and of the interactions between matter and radiation within celestial bodies and interstellar space.

Levels offered: Bachelor's, Master's, Doctoral.

Typical courses: Astronomical Optics, Relativistic Astrophysics, Particle Physics and the Very Early Universe, Interstellar matter, Radiation Measurement.

Related/complementary majors: Aerospace, Aeronautical, and Astronautical Engineering, Astronomy.

Needed abilities: excellent aptitude for physical science and mathematics, analytical ability.

Career possibilities: astronaut, astrophysicist.

Atmospheric Sciences and Meteorology

Describes the chemical and the physical properties of the mass of air surrounding the earth, and weather.

Levels offered: Bachelor's, Master's, Doctoral.

Typical courses: Climates of the Continents, Cloud Physics, Atmospheric Pollution, Weather Chart Analysis, Weather Observations Laboratory.

Related/complementary majors: Astronomy, Astrophysics, Chemistry, Physics.

Needed abilities: excellent aptitude for physical and chemical sciences, analytical ability.

Career possibilities: weather forecaster, weather researcher.

Atomic/Molecular Physics

Describes the properties and behavior of matter on the smallest scale at which chemical elements can be identified.

Levels offered: Master's, Doctoral.

Typical courses: Bohr Theory, Multi-Electron Atoms, Molecular Spectra, Hydrogen Atom.

Related/complementary majors: Physical Chemistry.

Needed abilities: excellent aptitude for physical science and mathematics, analytical ability.

Career possibilities: physicist.

Audiology/Auditory and Hearing Science

Prepares individuals for the nonmedical management of the auditory and balance systems.

Levels offered: Bachelor's, Master's, Doctoral.

Typical courses: Industrial Audiology and Hearing Conservation, Audiological Assessment Differential Diagnosis, Hearing Aid Selection, Calibration Instrumentation, Anatomy and Physiology of the Ear.

Related/complementary majors: Communication Disorders, Neuroscience.

Needed abilities: excellent aptitude for biological and physical science, analytical ability, problem-solving skills.

Career possibilities: audiology support technician, hearing aid dispenser, audiologist (with a doctoral degree).

Automotive Mechanics/Technology

Prepares individuals to engage in the service and maintenance of all types of automobiles.

Levels offered: Associate; limited number of Bachelor's.

Typical courses: Automotive Transmissions, Automotive Fuel and Emission Systems, Steering and Suspensions, Basic Electrical Systems.

Related/complementary majors: Diesel Engine Mechanics.

Needed abilities: excellent mechanical aptitude, analytical ability, problem-solving skills.

Career possibilities: auto technician, service writer, fleet manager.

Aviation Management

Prepares individuals in the nature and application of management methods and techniques related to the aviation industry.

Levels offered: Associate, Bachelor's, limited number of Master's.

Typical courses: Airport Management, Aviation Law, Airline Operations and Management, Passenger Operations, Supply and Distribution in the Airline Industry.

Related/complementary majors: Business Administration and Management.

Needed abilities: ability to understand and apply complex business principles to the aviation industry, analytical ability, problem-solving skills.

Career possibilities: airport manager, manager of airline operations.

Bacteriology

Describes the morphology, physiology, metabolism, and growth of bacteria, and their effects upon substances and other organisms.

Levels offered: Master's, Doctoral.

Typical courses: Bacterial Genetics, Physiology of Micro-Organisms, Microbial Metabolism, Host-Parasite Interactions, Food-Borne Disease Hazards.

Related/complementary majors: Biology, Botany, Microbiology, Pathology, Physiology.

Needed abilities: excellent scientific aptitude, analytical abilities.

Career possibilities: research scientist (with a graduate degree), scientific technician.

Banking and Financial Services

Prepares graduates for operating positions within financial institutions such as banks, savings and loans, credit unions, and investment firms.

Levels offered: Associate, Bachelor's.

Typical courses: Business Communication, Business Law, Money and Banking, Principles of Banking, Managerial Accounting.

Related/complementary majors: Business Administration and Management, Finance.

Needed abilities: excellent aptitude for business, analytical ability, problem-solving skills.

Career possibilities: bank teller, financial services customer service representative, credit union member associate.

Bible Studies

Describes the study of the interpretation and utilization of the Bible in the evolution of religious traditions.

Levels offered: Associate, Bachelor's, Master's, Doctoral.

Typical courses: Bible Geography, Biblical Themes, New Testament Survey, The Gospel of Luke, Old Testament Poetry.

Related/complementary majors: Biblical Languages, Religion, Theological Studies.

Needed abilities: aptitude for philosophy, history, and religious studies, analytical ability.

Career possibilities: religious educator, religious writer.

Bilingual Education

Describes the theories, methods, and techniques of designing, implementing, and evaluating programs which prepare, upgrade, or retrain students in English and another (their first) language.

Levels offered: Bachelor's, Master's, Doctoral.

Typical courses: Introduction to Bilingual Linguistics, Characteristics of Culturally Different Youth, Teaching Reading and Language Arts to Bilingual Students, Techniques for Teaching English as a Second Language in the Bicultural Classroom.

Related/complementary majors: Education (Elementary, Secondary, Adult), English, Foreign Languages, Linguistics.

Needed abilities: excellent communication and interpersonal skills, proficiency in a second language.

Career possibilities: bilingual teacher.

Biochemistry

Describes the chemistry of living systems and the biological phenomena that result from the interactions of these systems.

Levels offered: Bachelor's, Master's, Doctoral.

Typical courses: Physical Biochemistry of Macromolecules, Biological Ultrastructure, Bio-Organic Catalysis, Molecular Mechanisms of Development.

Related/complementary majors: Biology, Biophysics, Chemistry, Organic Chemistry.

Needed abilities: excellent aptitude for biology and chemistry, analytical ability.

Career possibilities: researcher, teacher.

Bioengineering and Biomedical Engineering

Describes the application of engineering and technological concepts, principles, and practices to human and other living systems.

Levels offered: Bachelor's, Master's, Doctoral.

Typical courses: Implant Materials, Ultrasonic Bioinstrumentation, Physics of Heat, Wave Motion, and Optics, Computer Applications in Engineering, Biomedical Systems, Electronic Devices, Circuits.

Related/complementary majors: Anatomy, Physiology, Physics.

Needed abilities: excellent aptitude for biology, physics, and mathematics, analytical ability, problem-solving skills.

Career possibilities: biomedical engineer.

Biology, General

Describes life forms, including the structure, function, reproduction, growth, heredity, evolution, behavior, and distribution of living organisms.

Levels offered: Associate, Bachelor's, Master's, Doctoral.

Typical courses: DNA structure, Anatomy, Cell Physiology, Virology, Botany.

Related/complementary majors: Botany, Ecology, Zoology.

Needed abilities: excellent aptitude for biological science, analytical ability.

Career possibilities: lab worker, medical sales representative, scientist, teacher.

Biomedical Electronics/Equipment Technology/ Biomedical Engineering Technology

Prepares individuals to manufacture, install, calibrate, operate, and maintain sophisticated life-support equipment found in hospitals, medical centers, and research labs, or the medical electronics industry.

Levels offered: Associate.

Typical courses: Biomedical Instrumentation, Biomedical Circuits and Devices, Introduction to Digital Electronics, Hospital and Patient Safety.

Related/complementary majors: Electrical Technology, Electronic Technology.

Needed abilities: good aptitude for applied mathematics, physics, and biomedical science, analytical skills, problem-solving skills, mechanical ability.

Career possibilities: biomedical equipment technician, medical equipment sales representative.

Biomedical Science

Describes a synthesis of basic clinical sciences with applied medical technology and research.

Levels offered: Master's, Doctoral.

Typical courses: Computer Applications in Basic Biomedical Science, Principles of Systems Analysis Applied to Biomedicine, Biostatistics, Lab Animal Science.

Related/complementary majors: Anatomy, Bioengineering/Biomedical Engineering, Biostatistics, Physiology.

Needed abilities: excellent aptitude for biological science, analytical ability.

Career possibilities: medical program monitor, researcher.

Biophysics

Describes biological phenomena using physical principles and methods.

Levels offered: Master's, Doctoral.

Typical courses: Biomedical Ultrasound, Lasers in Medicine, Medical Imaging, Computer Applications in Biomedical Science, Sonic Imaging and Signal Processing.

Related/complementary majors: Bioengineering and Biomedical Engineering, Biology, Physics.

Needed abilities: excellent aptitude for biological and physical sciences, analytical ability.

Career possibilities: biophysical researcher/inventor.

Biostatistics

Describes the application of mathematical and statistical models and methodology in biology.

Levels offered: Master's, Doctoral.

Typical courses: Computer Management of Health Data, Statistical Methods in Medical Studies, Sampling Methods for the Health Sciences, Applied Multivariate Biostatistics.

Related/complementary majors: Biology, Epidemiology, Public Health, Statistics.

Needed abilities: excellent aptitude for biological sciences and mathematics, analytical ability, orientation to detail.

Career possibilities: biological researcher, biostatistician.

Biotechnology

Describes the use of living organisms or their processes or output to make a product or solve a (medical, environmental, agricultural) problem.

Levels offered: Associate, Bachelors, Master's.

Typical courses: Tissue Culture Methods, Industrial Biotechnology, Quality Assurance in the Food Industry, Techniques in Protein Purification and Analysis.

Related/complementary majors: Biology, Engineering.

Needed abilities: strong aptitude for science, analytical ability, problem-solving skills.

Career possibilities: biotechnology aide, biotechnologist.

Botany, General

Describes the structure, function, reproduction, growth, heredity, evolution, and descriptions of plant life.

Levels offered: Bachelor's, Master's, Doctoral.

Typical courses: Elements of Plant Geography, Plant Biochemistry, Plant Anatomy, Plant Genetics, Plant Pathology.

Related/complementary majors: Horticulture, Plant Physiology.

Needed abilities: excellent aptitude for biological science, analytical ability.

Career possibilities: botanical researcher, greenhouse/nursery manager, marketing representative for a horticultural products form.

Broadcast Journalism

Describes the methods and techniques by which radio and television news programs are produced and broadcasted.

Levels offered: Bachelor's, Master's.

Typical courses: Radio-TV Speaking, Television Direction, Radio and Television News, Radio Writing, Fundamentals of Broadcasting.

Needed abilities: excellent oral and written communication skills, analytical ability.

Career possibilities: radio/television broadcaster or producer.

Business Administration and Management

Describes the planning, organizing, and controlling of a business, including organizational and human aspects, with emphasis on various theories of management, the knowledge and understanding necessary for managing people and functions, and decision making.

Levels offered: Associate, Bachelor's, Master's, Doctoral.

Typical courses: Financial Management, Managerial Economics, Marketing, Business Statistics, Business Communications.

Related/complementary majors: Accounting, Economics, Management Science.

Needed abilities: aptitude for all aspects of business, analytical ability, problem-solving skills.

Career possibilities: financial manager, investment broker, manager.

Business Economics

Describes the principles and methods for organizing a business firm and for combining resources to produce goods and services, taking account of costs, profits, and the nature and extent of competition in markets.

Levels offered: Bachelor's, Master's, Doctoral.

Typical courses: Econometrics, Business Cycles, Monetary and Fiscal Policy, Business Fluctuations and Forecasting, Labor Economics.

Related/complementary majors: Business Administration and Management, Economics, Logistics/Operations/Supply Chain Management.

Needed abilities: aptitude for business principles and practices, analytical ability, problem-solving skills.

Career possibilities: business owner/manager.

Business Education

Describes the theories, methods, and techniques in teaching business technology courses.

Levels offered: Bachelor's, Master's

Typical courses: Business Math, Office Procedures, Desktop Publishing, Records Management, Business Communications.

Related/complementary majors: Adult Education, Secondary Education.

Needed abilities: business technology skills, communication skills.

Career possibilities: business teacher.

Cardiovascular Technology

Prepares individuals to assist physicians in the evaluation, diagnosis, and treatment of cardiac patients.

Levels offered: Associate, Bachelor's.

Typical courses: Echocardiography, Cardiac Pathologies, Ultrasound Physics and Instrumentation, Cardiovascular Hemodynamics.

Related/complementary majors: Diagnostic Medical Sonography.

Needed abilities: aptitude for applied physics and physiology/anatomy, good interpersonal skills, ability to work precisely and to follow established standards under the direction of a physician.

Career possibilities: cardiovascular technologist.

Carpentry

Prepares individuals to fabricate, erect, install, and repair wooden structures and fixtures.

Levels offered: Associate.

Typical courses: Woodwork Fundamentals, Wood Finishing, Advanced Woodwork, Cabinet Construction.

Related/complementary majors: Construction.

Needed abilities: good visual perception, excellent manual dexterity, moderate physical agility, strength, and stamina, orientation to details, ability to work precisely, basic math skills.

Career possibilities: carpenter, construction foreman, contractor, lumber salesperson.

Cellular/Molecular Biology

Describes the cell as a unit of organization in plants and animals, and the molecular structure and processes of living organisms.

Levels offered: Master's, Doctoral.

Typical courses: Cell Proliferation and Oncogenic Viruses, Electron Microscopy Laboratory, Biosynthesis of Macromolecules, Cellular Regulation, Membranes and Bioenergetics.

Related/complementary majors: Biochemistry.

Needed abilities: excellent aptitude for biological science, strong analytical ability.

Career possibilities: research scientist.

Ceramic Engineering

Describes the techniques of designing, developing, and controlling processes that are involved in the manufacture of clay and ceramicware, porcelain, china, pottery, and related substances.

Levels offered: Bachelor's, Master's, Doctoral.

Typical courses: High Temperature Technology, Application of Statistics to Materials, Refractories, Ceramic Engineering Design, Thermochemistry.

Related/complementary majors: Materials Engineering.

Needed abilities: excellent aptitude for physical science and mathematics, analytical ability, problem-solving skills.

Career possibilities: ceramic engineer.

Ceramics

Describes methods of fashioning objects made of clay.

Levels offered: Bachelor's, Master's.

Typical courses: Advanced Clay Forming, Creative Problem Solving in Clay, Ceramic Sculpture, Kiln Building, Glazing and Firing Techniques.

Related/complementary majors: Sculpture.

Needed abilities: eye for visual detail, manual dexterity, creativity.

Career possibilities: ceramics artist, ceramics teacher.

Chemical Engineering

Describes the nature of chemical processes, heat and mass transfer, the handling and treatment of liquids and gases, and physical and physical-chemical operations.

Levels offered: Bachelor's, Master's, Doctoral.

Typical courses: Chemical Kinetics, Polymer Science, Chemical-Reaction Engineering, Fluid Dynamics, Instrumentation and Automatic Process Control.

Related/complementary majors: Physical Chemistry, Physics.

Needed abilities: excellent aptitude for chemistry, physics, and mathematics, analytical ability, problem-solving skills.

Career possibilities: chemical engineer.

Chemistry, General

Describes the micro and macro structure of matter, of the changes matter undergoes, of the energy involved in these changes, and of the models that interpret and the theories and laws that describe these phenomena.

Levels offered: Associate, Bachelor's, Master's, Doctoral.

Typical courses: Quantitative Analysis, Organic Chemistry, Instrumental Methods, Physical Chemistry.

Related/complementary majors: Biochemistry, Inorganic Chemistry, Organic Chemistry, Physical Chemistry.

Needed abilities: excellent aptitude for chemistry, analytical ability, orientation to details.

Career possibilities: chemist, quality control specialist, sales representative.

Child Life

Prepares individuals to work in hospitals and community health care settings with ill, injured, and disabled children and their families helping them cope with the realities of the medical situation and providing normal life experiences that optimize growth and development.

Levels offered: Bachelor's, Master's.

Typical courses: Child Development, Medical Aspects of Illness, Therapeutic Play Techniques, Child Life Program Development and Administration, Child Life in the Health care Setting: A Family-Oriented Approach.

Related/complementary majors: Early Childhood Education, Elementary Education, Developmental Psychology, Recreational Therapy, Exceptional Education.

Needed abilities: excellent communication skills, ability to empathize with children and their families, analytical ability, problem-solving skills.

Career possibilities: child life specialist.

Chiropractic Medicine

Describes the principles and techniques (such as manipulation of the spinal column) for relieving disorders caused by abnormal function of the nervous system.

Levels offered: Doctoral.

Typical courses: Cervical Techniques, Palpation, Topographical Anatomy, Introduction to X-ray, Neuromusculoskeletal Pathology.

Related/complementary majors: Anatomy, Neurosciences, Physical Therapy, Physiology, Sports Medicine.

Needed abilities: excellent aptitude for applied biological and physical sciences, good interpersonal skills, analytical ability, problem-solving skills, good manual dexterity, good physical strength and stamina.

Career possibilities: chiropractor.

Church/Religious Music

Focuses on the role of music in religion.

Levels offered: Associate (limited number of programs), Bachelor's, Master's, Doctoral (limited number of programs).

Typical courses: Practice of Church Music, Oratorio Chorus, Philosophy of Church Music, Church Music Education.

Related/complementary majors: Music Performance, Music

Theory and Composition, Religious Education, Theological Professions.

Needed abilities: musical aptitude on piano/voice/organ composition, ability to apply religious techniques and practices.

Career possibilities: choir director, church musician, religious music composer.

Civil Engineering

Describes the conception, analysis, design, testing, construction, and operation of structures, transportation components and systems, water resources and conveyance systems, pollution control systems, water treatment systems, and appurtenant works.

Levels offered: Bachelor's, Master's, Doctoral.

Typical courses: Dynamics of Structures and earthquake Engineering, Traffic Control Systems, Concrete and Asphalt Behavior, Water Quality Analysis, Viscous Flow Theory.

Related/complementary majors: Environmental Technology, Physics, Urban Design.

Needed abilities: excellent aptitude for physical science and mathematics, analytical ability, problem-solving skills.

Career possibilities: civil engineer

Civil Engineering Technology

Prepares individuals to assist a civil engineer in design, surveying, controlling materials, testing, and building of structures.

Levels offered: Associate, Bachelor's.

Typical courses: Strength of Materials, Contracts and Specifications, Blueprint Reading, Drafting, Surveying.

Related/complementary majors: Architectural Technology, Construction, Drafting and Design Technology, Surveying and Mapping Technology.

Needed abilities: aptitude for applied physics and mathematics, analytical ability, problem-solving skills, orientation to detail.

Career possibilities: building inspector, civil engineer technician, construction manager.

Classical Studies

Describes the language and literature of the ancient Greco-Roman world in English translation.

Levels offered: Bachelor's, Master's, Doctoral.

Typical courses: Greek and Roman Language and Literature, Greek Tragedy, Latin Prose, Plato, Roman Satire.

Related/complementary majors: Comparative Literature, History, Humanities, Languages (Classical Greek or Latin).

Needed abilities: verbal aptitude for reading and understanding ancient literature and languages, analytical ability.

Career possibilities: Teacher.

Clinical Psychology

Describes the application of appropriate methods and theories for the assessment, prevention, and treatment of psychological distress, disability, dysfunctional behavior, and the enhancement of psychological well-being.

Levels offered: Master's, Doctoral.

Typical courses: Behavior Modification with Adults, Psychotherapy with Adolescents, Family Dynamics and Therapy, Advanced Clinical Assessment, Psychological Problems of Children.

Related/complementary majors: Counseling Psychology.

Needed abilities: excellent aptitude for psychological science, excellent interpersonal skills, analytical skills, problem-solving skills.

Career possibilities: clinical psychologist.

Cognitive Psychology

Describes the acquisition and recall of new behaviors, and of the processes of learning new activities, and of retaining them over time.

Levels offered: Master's, Doctoral.

Typical courses: Psycholinguistics, Human Information Processing, Quantitative Methods in Cognitive Psychology, Human Learning and Memory, Perception.

Related/complementary majors: Educational Psychology, Experimental Psychology, Education, Neuroscience.

Needed abilities: excellent aptitude for psychological science, analytical ability, problem-solving skills.

Career possibilities: research psychologist, educational consultant.

Communications

Describes the creation, transmission, and evaluation of messages.

Levels offered: Associate, Bachelor's, Master's, Doctoral.

Typical courses: Small Group Communication, Communication, Power and Values, Analysis of Verbal Communication, Communication Theory, Sociolinguistics.

Related/complementary majors: Advertising, Journalism, Public Relations, Radio/Television.

Needed abilities: aptitude for verbal or visual expression, creativity.

Career possibilities: advertising employee, journalist/writer, public relations manager, radio/television worker.

Communications Disorders

Describes the theory and practice of managing any disorder that impairs language abilities in terms of speaking, hearing, or other aspects of communication with others.

Levels offered: Bachelor's, Master's, Doctoral.

Typical courses: Language Assessment of Communication Disorders, Voice and Fluency Disorders, Introduction to Audiology, Anatomy and Physiology of Speech Processes, Normal Language Acquisition.

Related/complementary majors: Speech Pathology and Audiology, Education of the Deaf and Hearing Impaired.

Needed abilities: aptitude for biological (anatomy and physiology) science, excellent interpersonal skills, analytical ability, problem-solving skills.

Career possibilities: speech pathology assistant (bachelor's degree), speech therapist (master's), researcher/master clinician/college professor (doctoral).

Community College Education Administration

Describes the principles and techniques of planning, organizing, developing, staffing, coordinating, managing, researching, evaluating, financing, and controlling junior and community college institutions.

Levels offered: Master's, Doctoral.

Typical courses: Occupational Education, Developmental and Remedial Education, Contemporary Issues in Community Colleges, Community College Finance, Instructional Strategies for Community College Teachers.

Related/complementary majors: Adult Education, Higher Education Administration.

Needed abilities: ability to coordinate educational theories and practices with management principles, analytical ability, problem-solving skills, managerial skills.

Career possibilities: community college administrator.

Community Psychology

Describes the theory and practices of using psychology in the broader social community, working with private and public organizations.

Levels offered: Master's, Doctoral.

Typical courses: Research in Community Psychology, Community Organizing, Behavioral Change, Consultation.

Related/complementary majors: Industrial/Organizational Psychology, Social Psychology, Social Work, Sociology.

Needed abilities: excellent aptitude for psychological science, analytical ability, problem-solving skills, communication skills.

Career possibilities: psychologist, consultant.

Comparative Literature

Describes the comparison of various aspects of literature, based on selected dimensions such as genre, theme, literary period, and language source.

Levels offered: Bachelor's, Master's, Doctoral.

Typical courses: Medieval Literature, Comedy in Film and Literature, Women in Literature, Japanese Literature.

Related/complementary majors: Literature (American, British), Foreign Language.

Needed abilities: good ear and eye for written language, analytical ability.

Career possibilities: editor, library assistant, writer.

Computational Biology/Bioinformatics

Describes computational approaches to analyze patterns in biological data to create complex models of biological activities, including functions of genes and their interactions.

Levels offered: Bachelor's, Master's, Doctoral

Typical courses: Microarray Methodology and Analysis, Research Ethics, Biometrics, Gene Expression Analysis, Advanced Algorithms.

Related/complementary majors: Biochemistry, Biology, Computer Science, Statistics.

Needed abilities: strong aptitude for biological science, math, and computer science; analytical ability.

Career possibilities: bioinformaticist, research scientist, lab technician.

Computer/Digital Animation

Describes the planning, production, and concepts behind 3-D computer-generated animation.

Levels offered: Associate, Bachelor's, Master's.

Typical courses: History of Animation, Drawing for Animation, Film Language and Visual Storytelling, Animation Pre-Production, Concept/Character/Environment.

Related/complementary courses: Drawing, Film.

Needed abilities: eye for artistic detail, creativity, computer literacy.

Career possibilities: animator, technical director, modeler.

Computer Engineering

Describes the study of computer hardware and software, with an emphasis on design and application to engineering disciplines.

Levels offered: Bachelor's, Master's, Doctoral.

Typical courses: Digital Systems Design, Data Structures, Computer Architecture, Embedded Systems, Electronics.

Related/complementary majors: Computer Science, Electronics Engineering, Electrical Engineering.

Needed abilities: excellent aptitude for math and physical science, analytical ability, problem-solving skills, creativity.

Career possibilities: computer engineer/designer.

Computer Science

Describes the study of the hardware and software of computers, and its use as a tool in various disciplines.

Levels offered: Bachelor's, Master's, Doctoral.

Typical courses: Software Development and Systems, Programming Languages, Introduction to Computer Algorithms, Ethical and Societal Issues in Computer Science.

Related/complementary courses: Information Science, Mathematics, Computer Engineering.

Needed abilities: excellent aptitude for technology, mathematics, and logical thinking, analytical ability, problem-solving skills.

Career possibilities: computer technician, software developer.

Computer Technology

Describes the application of computing equipment and methods to solve human and business problems.

Levels offered: Associate.

Typical courses: Introduction to Operating Systems, Visual Basic Programming, Fundamentals of Network Security, Technical Support and Diagnostics.

Related/complementary majors: Electronics Technology, Information Science.

Career possibilities: technical support, network administrator, computer technician.

Conducting

Provides training for students to become professional conductors.

Levels offered: Master's, Doctoral.

Typical courses: Studies in Choral Repertoire, Studies in Wind Ensemble/Band Repertoire, Studies in Orchestra/Opera Repertoire, Advanced Studies and Directed Performance in Conducting.

Related/complementary majors: Music Performance, Music Composition.

Needed abilities: excellent aptitude for music.
Career possibilities: conductor.

Conflict/Dispute Analysis/Management/ Resolution

Prepares individuals to design, practice, and evaluate personal, professional, organizational, and societal conflict resolution applications in a nonviolent and nonlitigious manner.

Levels offered: Master's, Doctoral.

Typical courses: Negotiation Theory and Practice, Interpersonal and Intergroup Conflict, Violence Prevention and Intervention, Theories and Philosophies of Conflict and Peace, Family Mediation Skills Training.

Related/complementary majors: Human Resources, International Affairs, Peace Studies, Political Science, Psychology, Sociology, Labor/Industrial Relations.

Needed abilities: Strong aptitude for social science, excellent communication skills, ability to see both sides of an issue.

Career possibilities: arbitrator, facilitator, mediator, negotiator.

Conservation Biology

Describes the scientific study of how to maintain and restore habitats and protect wildlife.

Levels offered: Bachelor's, Master's, Doctoral.

Typical courses: Evolution and Extinction, Economic and Social Aspects of Conservation Biology, Contemporary Problems in Conservation Biology, Habitats and Regulation of Wildlife.

Related/complementary majors: Wildlife Management, Plant Protection, Fisheries, Marine Biology.

Needed abilities: excellent aptitude for biological science, some aptitude for social science and economics.

Career possibilities: environmental educator, naturalist, park ranger, game warden.

Construction/Management

Prepares individuals to erect, install, maintain, and repair residential or industrial structures.

Levels offered: Associate, Bachelor's, Master's.

Typical courses: Construction Estimating, Construction Contracts and Law, Electrical Systems in Construction, Construction Building Codes.

Related/complementary majors: Business Administration and Management, Air Conditioning, Heating and Refrigeration Technology, Architectural Technology, Carpentry, Civil Engineering.

Needed abilities: moderate aptitude for applied physics and mathematics, orientation for details, mechanical aptitude, aptitude for business principles and practices.

Career possibilities: construction estimator, construction foreman, general contractor, inspector.

Counseling Psychology

Describes the theory and practices of systematically selecting the facts and theories of psychology with the intent of advising people about their problems.

Levels offered: Master's, Doctoral.

Typical courses: Psychopathology Through Adult Life, Psychodynamic Psychotherapy and Counseling, Career Development: Theory and Counseling, Group Dynamics, Systems pf Group, Marital and Family Therapy.

Related/complementary majors: Clinical Psychology, Developmental Psychology.

Needed abilities: excellent interpersonal skills, excellent aptitude for behavioral science, analytical ability, problem-solving skills.

Career possibilities: career counselor, marriage and family counselor, psychologist.

Court Reporting

Prepares individuals to record examination, testimony, judicial opinions, judge's charge to jury, judgment or sentence of court, or other proceedings in a court of law by using machine shorthand.

Levels offered: associate.

Typical courses: Court Orientation, Machine Shorthand, Law for the Court Reporter, Legal Terminology and Transcription, Business English.

Related/complementary majors: Legal Assisting/Secretarial.

Needed abilities: excellent keyboarding speed, orientation for details, ability to work precisely, good listening skills, good spelling ability, ability to master technical (medical/legal terminology).

Career possibilities: court reporter.

Creative Writing

Describes the techniques of composition of such forms as literature as the short story, verse. drama, and others that involve some degree of spontaneity and exercise of the imagination on the of the writer.

Levels offered: Bachelor's, Master's, Doctoral.

Typical courses: The Short Story, Children's Literature, Scriptwriting, Advanced Poetry Writing.

Related/complementary majors: English.

Needed ability: excellent writing skills, creativity.

Career possibilities: novel writer, script writer.

Criminal Justice

Describes the principles and procedures of developing, administering, and managing correctional, law enforcement, and forensic services.

Levels offered: Bachelor's, Master's, Doctoral.

Typical courses: Police and Community Relations, Civil Disobedience, Urban Violence and Dissent, Juvenile Delinquency, Criminal Justice Planning and Research, Criminal Law.

Related/complementary majors: Criminology, Forensic Studies, law Enforcement, Public Administration.

Needed abilities: aptitude for social science, applied legal principles, and management techniques, analytical ability, problem-solving skills.

Career possibilities: corrections officer, probation/parole officer, criminal justice administrator.

Criminal Justice Technology

Prepares individuals for entry-level work in law enforcement, corrections, and criminal justice.

Levels offered: Associate.

Typical courses: Police and Patrol Procedures, Vehicle Codes and Traffic Investigation, Criminal Investigations, Criminal and Related Law.

Related/complementary majors: Law Enforcement.

Needed abilities: good interpersonal skills, analytical ability, ability to follow established procedures.

Career possibilities: police officer, bailiff, corrections officer.

Criminology

Describes the causes of crime and the methods of dealing with crime and the criminal, including crime statistics, theories of punishment, and the role of law enforcement in society as an agent for the prevention and treatment of crime.

Levels offered: Bachelor's, Master's, Doctoral.

Typical courses: Civil Liberties, Penology, Juvenile Delinquency, law Enforcement, Social Statistical Methods.

Related/complementary majors: Criminal Justice, Psychology, Sociology.

Needed abilities: excellent aptitude for social science, analytical ability.

Career possibilities: crime researcher/analyst, criminal justice administrator.

Culinary Arts

Provides students with practical instruction in food production and cooking.

Levels offered: Associate, Bachelor's (very limited number).

Typical courses: Special Functions Operations, Foods of Asia, Stocks, Sauces, and Soups, Classical French Cuisine, Nutritional and Sensory Analysis.

Related/complementary majors: Restaurant Management.

Needed abilities: creativity, good manual dexterity, aptitude for business management.

Career possibilities: chef, food service manager.

Curriculum and Instruction

Describes the theories, methods, and procedures of designing, controlling, developing, and integrating educational activities and programs.

Levels offered: Master's, Doctoral.

Typical courses: Language, Reading, and Writing, Computers and Curriculum, Research in Reading, Curriculum Development.

Related/complementary majors: Education (Early Childhood, Elementary, Middle, Secondary, Adult, Special).

Needed abilities: aptitude for education practices and principles, analytical ability, problem-solving skills.

Career possibilities: curriculum writer, educational materials developer.

Cytotechnology

Prepares individuals to stain, mount, and screen slides of cells of the human body for determination of abnormalities.

Levels offered: Bachelor's.

Typical courses: Pulmonary and Gastric Cytology, Pathology of the Female Genital Tract, Cellular Morphology, Microscopy and Laboratory Techniques, Cytogenetics.

Related/complementary majors: Biology, Medical Technology.

Needed abilities: strong aptitude for biology, good visual perception, orientation to details, ability to work precisely and follow established procedures.

Career possibilities: cytotechnologist.

Dairy

Describes the theories, principles, and applications of appropriate technical skills that apply to the production of milk animals and dairy products.

Levels offered: Associate, Bachelor's, Master's, Doctoral.

Typical courses: Dairy Cattle Judging, Applied Dairy Cattle Nutrition, Dairy Calf Management, Dairy Reproduction.

Related majors: Agriculture/Business, Animal Science.

Needed abilities: aptitude for biological science and applied business principles and practices, analytical ability, problem-solving skills.

Career possibilities: agricultural extension specialist, manager of a dairy farm.

Dance

Describes the performance and choreography of various kinds of dance, including ballet, modern, jazz, ethnic, and folk dance.

Levels offered: Associate, Bachelor's, Master's, Doctoral.

Typical courses: Dance History, Research in Dance Kinesiology, Choreography, Essentials of Ballet Teaching, Pointe.

Related/complementary majors: Dance Therapy, Music History and Appreciation.

Needed abilities: Superior dance ability, aptitude for kinesiology, excellent physical stamina, creativity.

Career possibilities: dancer, dance teacher, choreographer.

Dance/Movement Therapy

Prepares individuals to apply the principles and techniques of dance and related movement to the rehabilitation of mentally and physically challenged individuals.

Levels offered: Master's.

Typical courses: Movement Therapy with Children, Dance, Movement, and Human Behavior, The Expressive Arts and Mental Health, Dance Therapy for Geriatric Populations.

Related/complementary majors: Dance, Music Therapy, Occupational Therapy, Recreational Therapy, Physical Therapy, Psychology.

Career possibilities: dance therapist.

Deaf Studies

Provides mastery of sign language and critical insight into deaf culture.

Levels offered: Bachelor's, Master's, Doctoral.

Typical courses: History of the Deaf Community, Psychology and Deaf People, Deaf Women's Studies, The Deaf in Literature, Sociology of Deafness and Deaf People.

Related/complementary majors: Communication Disorders, Sign Language Interpreting, Education of the Deaf and Hearing Impaired, Human Services.

Needed abilities: aptitude for social science, signing skills.

Career possibilities: interpreter or other professional who works with the hearing impaired.

Decision Science

Prepares students for decision-making, management, and consulting roles in nonprofit organizations, government, and business through understanding of individual and group behavior, rational decision-making, and organization of resources to make needed decisions.

Levels offered: Bachelor's, Master's, Doctoral.

Typical courses: Intelligent Decision Support Systems, Benefit-Cost Analysis, Social Decision Making, Ethical Judgments in Professional Life.

Related/complementary majors: Industrial and Organizational Psychology, Management Science.

Needed abilities: analytical thinking, problem-solving skills.

Career possibilities: analyst, manager.

Dental Assisting

Prepares individuals to assist a dentist in dental operations, to perform selected lab functions, and assist in office work.

Levels offered: Associate.

Typical courses: Dental Office Management, Dental Health Education, Dental Materials, Dental Radiology, Chairside Dental Assisting.

Related/complementary majors: Medical Assisting.

Needed aptitudes: moderate aptitude for applied biology, chemistry, and physics, good manual dexterity, excellent interpersonal skills, orientation to details, ability to work precisely under the direction of a dentist.

Career possibilities: dental assistant.

Dental Hygiene

Prepares individuals to provide chairside services to patients (such as performing complete oral prophylaxis) and to provide dental health education services to individuals and community health programs under the supervision of a dentist.

Levels offered: Associate, Bachelor's, Master's.

Typical courses: Oral Medicine, Periodontics Seminar, Radiology, Introduction to Patient Care, Dental Anatomy and Morphology.

Related/complementary majors: Public Health.

Needed abilities: good aptitude for biological and physical sciences, good interpersonal skills, good manual dexterity, orientation to details, ability to work precisely and to follow established standards, ability to work both independently and under the supervision of a dentist.

Career possibilities: dental hygienist.

Dental Laboratory Technology

Levels offered: Associate, Bachelor's (limited number).

Typical courses: Complete Dentures, Dental Ceramics, Dental Morphology, Orthodontics, Dental Metallurgy.

Related/complementary majors: Dental Assisting.

Needed abilities: excellent manual dexterity, excellent visual perception, orientation for details, ability to work precisely, ability to follow procedures prescribed by dentist.

Career possibilities: dental lab technician, dental supplies sales representative.

Dentistry

Describes the prevention, diagnosis, and treatment of diseases of the teeth, gums, and oral structures.

Levels offered: Doctoral.

Typical courses: Oral Diagnosis, Oral Surgery, Diagnostic Orthodontics, Operative Dentistry, Dental Public Health.

Related/complementary majors: Anatomy, Physiology.

Needed abilities: excellent aptitude for the biological and physical sciences, excellent manual dexterity, orientation to detail, good interpersonal skills, analytical ability, problem-solving skills.

Career possibilities: dentist.

Developmental Psychology

Describes the progressive changes in the behavioral process of individuals as a function of aging through the life span, from conception to death.

Levels offered: Master's, Doctoral.

Typical courses: Perceptual Development, Personality Development of the Adolescent, Psychology of Death and Dying, Cognitive Development, Development of Language and Communication.

Related/complementary majors: Individual and Family Development, Psychobiology.

Needed abilities: excellent aptitude for psychosocial science, analytical ability.

Career possibilities: counselor, psychological researcher, psychology writer.

Diagnostic Medical Sonography

Prepares individuals to use sound waves to generate an image for the assessment and diagnosis of medical conditions.

Levels offered: Associate, Bachelor's (limited number of programs).

Typical courses: Ultrasound Instrumentation, Ultrasound Physics, Ultrasound Cross-Sectional Anatomy, Obstetrical Ultrasound.

Related/complementary majors: Anatomy, Physiology, Radiologic Technology.

Needed abilities: aptitude for applied physics and physiology/anatomy, good interpersonal skills, ability to work precisely and to follow established standards under the direction of a physician.

Career possibilities: ultrasound technician.

Diesel Engine Mechanics/Technology

Prepares individuals to repair diesel engines in vehicles such as buses, ships, trucks, railroad locomotives, and construction equipment.

Levels offered: Associate.

Typical courses: Fuel Injection, Brake Systems, Basic Electrical Laboratory, Transmission Repair, Air Conditioning.

Related/complementary majors: Auto Technology.

Needed abilities: mechanical aptitude, analytical ability, problem-solving skills.

Career possibilities: diesel mechanic.

Dietetic Technology

Prepares individuals to assist dietitians in the application of food and nutrition to health.

Levels offered: Associate.

Typical courses: Menu Management, Cultural Considerations in Nutrition and Healthcare, Introduction to Diet Therapy, Principles of Nutrition.

Related/complementary courses: Biology.

Needed abilities: Moderate aptitude for biological science.

Career possibilities: dietetic technician, dietetic food service manager.

Digital Media Production Technology

Prepares individuals to work in the digital media industry.

Levels offered: Associate, Bachelor's.

Typical courses: Basic Animation, Digital Media Portfolio, Streaming Media, Advanced Web Page Creation, Planning and Management of Digital Media Authoring.

Related/complementary majors: Graphic Design, Entertainment Technology.

Needed abilities: ability to learn technology, creativity.

Career possibilities: digital media designer/producer/manager.

Drafting and Design Technology

Prepares individuals to assist mechanical, electrical and electronic, architectural, civil, mechanical, or other engineers and architects in the design and drafting of electrical circuits, machines, structures, weldments, or architectural plans.

Levels offered: Associate.

Typical courses: Technical Drawing, Fundamentals of Designing, Introduction to Computer-Aided Drafting, Materials Selection, Drafting Mechanics.

Related/complementary majors: Architectural Technology, Civil

Technology, Construction, Electronic Technology, Industrial Technology, Manufacturing Technology.

Needed abilities: excellent visual-spatial perception, analytical ability, orientation for details, ability to work precisely and according to standards established by architects or engineers.

Career possibilities: drafter.

Dramatic Arts

Describes the development, theory, and processes of creating live performances through human expressive modalities.

Levels offered: Associate, Bachelor's, Master's, Doctoral.

Typical courses: Theatre Production, Art of Directing, Acting Styles, Acting for the Camera, Drama Survey: Comedy.

Related/complementary majors: Film, Theatre Design.

Needed abilities: strong aptitude for one or more areas of the dramatic arts (acting/directing/producing/stage management), creativity.

Career possibilities: actor, writer, producer.

Drawing

Describes the aesthetic qualities, techniques, and creative processes of communicating ideas, feelings, and inner vision through representation of lines.

Levels offered: Associate, Bachelor's, Master's.

Typical courses: Chalk Pastel Drawing, Problems in Figure Drawing, Nature Drawing, Drawing Media and Technique, Structure and Color in Drawing.

Related/complementary majors: Art History and Appreciation, Painting, Graphic Design, Studio Art.

Needed abilities: eye for artistic detail, excellent manual dexterity, creativity.

Career possibilities: artist, illustrator.

Early Childhood Education

Describes the theories, methods, and techniques of designing, implementing, and evaluating organized learning and developmental activities for children from birth to age eight.

Levels offered: Associate, Bachelor's, Master's, Doctoral.

Typical courses: Child Development, Early Child Nutrition and Health, Children's Literature, Early Childhood Curriculum, Development and Learning through Play.

Related/complementary majors: Developmental Psychology.

Needed abilities: excellent communication skills, patience and energy for young children and their parents, analytical ability, problem-solving skills.

Career possibilities: early childhood teacher, child development specialist.

Earth Science

Describes the origin and structure of the earth.

Levels offered: Associate, Bachelor's, Master's, Doctoral.

Typical courses: Volcanology, Principles of Stratigraphy, Minerals and Rocks, Climate, Mineral Chemistry and Physics.

Related/complementary majors: Geology, Geochemistry, Geophysics and Seismology, Oceanography, Chemistry, Physics, Biology.

Needed abilities: strong aptitude for physical science, analytical ability.

Career possibilities: scientist/technician.

Ecology

Describes the interrelationships among organisms and their environments.

Levels offered: Bachelor's, Master's, Doctoral.

Typical courses: Population and Community Ecology, Ecology of Forest Fungi, Marine Ecology, Plant Ecology, Watershed Ecology.

Related/complementary majors: Biology, Conservation Biology, Forestry, Marine Biology, Plant and Soil Sciences, Zoology.

Needed abilities: excellent aptitude for natural science (especially biology), analytical ability, problem-solving skills.

Career possibilities: conservationist, environmental worker.

Economics

Describes the transformation of limited resources into goods and services which, upon distribution, are again transformed by consumption to yield satisfaction of human wants.

Levels offered: Bachelor's, Master's, Doctoral.

Typical courses: History of Economic Doctrines, Monetary Theory and Policy, Asian Economic Theory and Development, Capitalism and Socialism, Labor Market Analysis.

Related/complementary majors: Business Administration and Management, Business Economics, International Business Management.

Needed abilities: aptitude for complex business principles and practices, analytical ability.

Career possibilities: banker, economic analyst, stockbroker/investment advisor.

Education Administration and Supervision

Describes principles and techniques of planning, organizing, developing, staffing, coordinating, managing, researching, evaluating, financing, and controlling educational institutions and agencies.

Levels offered: Master's, Doctoral.

Typical courses: Program Design in Education, Politics of Education, Legal Research in Education, Decision Methods for Education Policy Managers.

Related/complementary majors: Education (Pre-Elementary/Elementary/Junior High/Secondary/Special Education).

Needed abilities: strong background in and understanding of educational practices and principles, versatility and capability for various management tasks.

Career possibilities: department head, principal.

Education of the Deaf and Hearing Impaired

Describes the theories, methods, and techniques of designing, implementing, and evaluating organized learning activities for students with hearing impairments that adversely affect their performance.

Levels offered: Bachelor's, Master's, Doctoral.

Typical courses: Reading Methods for the Hearing Impaired,

Psycholinguistics of Manual Communication, Language Methods for the Hearing Impaired, Learning Styles of the Hearing Impaired.

Related/complementary majors: Sign Language Interpretation, Speech Pathology and Audiology.

Needed abilities: excellent interpersonal and communication (including signing) skills, analytical ability, problem-solving skills.

Career possibilities: teacher of the hearing impaired.

Education of the Emotionally Impaired/ Behaviorally Disordered

Describes the theories, methods, and techniques of designing, implementing, and evaluating organized learning activities for students with emotional, behavioral, or interpersonal problems.

Levels offered: Bachelor's, Master's, Doctoral.

Typical courses: Diagnosis and Assessment in Emotional Disorders, Curriculum Practices for Children with Emotional Handicaps, Language and Reading Disorders in the Emotionally Disturbed, Psychopathology and Developmental Disabilities of Emotional Disorders.

Related/complementary courses: Exceptional Student Education, Psychology.

Needed abilities: excellent interpersonal and communication skills, analytical ability, problem-solving skills.

Career possibilities: teacher of students with behavioral and emotional disabilities.

Education of the Gifted and Talented

Describes the theories, methods, and techniques of designing, implementing, and evaluating organized learning activities for students capable of high performance, including those with demonstrated achievement or ability in any one or more of these areas: general intellectual ability, specific academic aptitude, creativity, leadership ability, visual and performing arts, or psychomotor ability.

Levels offered: Master's, Doctoral.

Typical courses: Nature and Needs of Gifted Children, Assessment of Exceptional Individuals, Social and Emotional Components of Giftedness, Instructional Processes for Gifted Children.

Related/complementary majors: specialized area of education, such as art, music, mathematics, or science.

Needed abilities: excellent interpersonal and communication skills, analytical ability, problem-solving skills.

Career possibilities: teacher of the gifted and talented.

Education of the Mentally Handicapped

Describes the theories, methods, and techniques of designing, implementing, and evaluating organized learning activities for students whose impaired mental development adversely affects their education performance.

Levels offered: Bachelor's, Master's, Doctoral.

Typical courses: Characteristics of the Mentally Retarded, Teaching the Mentally Challenged, Vocational Education for the Mentally Handicapped, Behavior Management of the Exceptional Individual.

Related/complementary majors: Education (Elementary, Secondary, Exceptional/Special).

Needed abilities: exceptional interpersonal and communication skills, analytical ability, problem-solving skills.

Career possibilities: special educator.

Education of the Physically Handicapped

Describes the theories, methods, and techniques of designing, implementing, and evaluating organized learning activities for students who have severe physical impairments that adversely affect their educational performance.

Levels offered: Bachelor's, Master's, Doctoral.

Typical courses: Technology for Children, Introduction to Biomechanics, Career Development of Exceptional Youth, Neurological and Orthopedic Dysfunction.

Related/complementary majors: Education.

Needed abilities: excellent interpersonal skills and communication skills, analytical ability, problem-solving skills.

Career possibilities: teacher of the physically handicapped.

Education of the Visually Handicapped

Describes the theories, methods, and techniques of designing, implementing, and evaluating organized learning activities for students who have a visual impairment that adversely affects their educational performance.

Levels offered: Bachelor's, Master's, Doctoral.

Typical courses: Working with the Low Vision Child, Teaching Reading to the Visually Handicapped, Visual Function and Dysfunction, Orientation and Mobility Instruction.

Needed abilities: excellent interpersonal and communication skills, analytical ability, problem-solving skills.

Career possibilities: teacher/rehabilitation instructor of the visually impaired.

Educational Psychology

Describes the theories and methods utilized to improve all the elements of teaching and learning.

Levels offered: Master's, Doctoral.

Typical courses: Cognitive Development Theory, Applied Psycholinguistics, Adaptive Instruction, Psychology of Motivation.

Related/complementary majors: Curriculum and Instruction, Education (Pre-Elementary/Elementary/Middle School/Secondary/Special Education), School Psychology, Cognitive Psychology.

Needed abilities: excellent aptitude for educational theory and psychology, analytical ability, problem solving skills.

Career possibilities: educational psychologist.

Electrical/Electronic/Communications Engineering

Describes the theory and practical application of electrical and electronic systems and their components, including circuits, electromagnetic fields, and energy sources.

Levels offered: Bachelor's, Master's, Doctoral.

Typical courses: Digital Control Systems, Numerical Techniques in Electromagnetics, Quantum Electronics and lasers, Microcomputer System Design, Integrated Circuit Design.

Related/complementary majors: Computer Engineering, Physics.

Needed abilities: excellent aptitude for mathematics and physics, analytical ability, problem-solving skills.

Career possibilities: electrical/electronics engineer.

Electromechanical Technology

Prepares individuals to assist mechanical and electrical engineers in the design, development, and testing of electromechanical devices and systems such as plant automation, automated control systems, servomechanisms, vending machines, elevator controls, missile controls, tape-control machines, and auxiliary computer equipment.

Levels offered: Associate.

Typical courses: Electrical Circuits, Machine and Electrical Drafting, Digital Computer Fundamentals, Electronic Theory, Mechanisms and Machine Design.

Related/complementary majors: Drafting and Design Technology, Electrical Technology, Electronic Technology.

Needed abilities: aptitude for applied physics and technology, analytical ability, problem-solving skills, ability to work under the direction of an engineer.

Career possibilities: electromechanical technician, engineering assistant.

Electroneurodiagnostic (END) Technology

Trains multiskilled allied health technologists who can perform electrodiagnostic tests on patients nervous and muscular systems to produce interpretable records of electroencephalography (EEG), evoked potentials (EP), nerve conduction velocity tests (NCV), electromyography (EMG), polysomnography (PSG), and interoperative monitoring (IOM).

Levels offered: Associate.

Typical courses: Neuroanatomy and Physiology, Basic EEG, Technical Electronics, Introduction to Physics, Advanced Evoked Potentials.

Related/complementary majors: Biology, Medical Assisting, Health Studies.

Needed abilities: moderate aptitude for biological and physical science, ability to operate technical equipment.

Career possibilities: END technician.

Electronic Game Design and Development

Prepares students for all levels of electronic (such as computer and video) game development, from the initial concept to the end product.

Levels offered: Associate, Bachelor's.

Typical courses: Game Concept Design, 3D Modeling, Applied Game Theory, History of Electronic Games, Game Tools and Techniques.

Related/complementary majors: Software Engineering, Digital Media.

Needed abilities: math skills, technical aptitude, creativity, analytical ability, problem-solving skills.

Career possibilities: electronic game designer/developer.

Electronic Technology

Prepares individuals to support the electronic engineer and other professionals in the design, development, modification, and testing of electronic circuits, devices, and systems.

Levels offered: Associate.

Typical courses: Circuit Applications Theory, Semiconductor Laboratory, Digital Systems Fundamentals, Electronic Prototype Fabrication, Structured Programming for Electronics.

Related/complementary majors: Computer Science, Physics.

Needed abilities: strong aptitude for applied physical science, good aptitude for mathematics, analytical ability, strong problem-solving skills.

Career possibilities: electronics technician.

Elementary Education

Describes the theories, methods, and techniques of designing, implementing, and evaluating organized learning activities at the elementary education level.

Levels offered: Bachelor's, Master's, Doctoral.

Typical courses: Problems and Principles of Elementary Education, Teaching of Science in Elementary Education, Directed Teaching in the Elementary Grades, Developmental Reading and Writing Instruction in Elementary Schools.

Related/complementary majors: Curriculum and Instruction.

Needed abilities: excellent interpersonal skills and communication skills, analytical ability, problem-solving skills.

Career possibilities: elementary educator.

Emergency Medical Technology

Prepares individuals to provide pre-hospital medical care to patients of all ages.

Levels offered: Associate, Bachelor's (limited number).

Typical courses: Pathophysiology and Management of Respiratory Emergencies, Emotional Aspects of Illness and Injury, Telemetry and EMS Communications, Paramedic Procedures, Advanced Life Support.

Related/complementary courses: Nursing, Physician Assisting, Physiology, Respiratory Therapy/Technology.

Needed abilities: strong aptitude for applied medical science, good interpersonal skills, ability to work under extreme pressure, good manual dexterity, physical strength and stamina, analytical ability, problem-solving skills, ability to work independently (using own judgment) and under the direction of a physician.

Career possibilities: emergency medical technician/paramedic.

Endocrinology

Describes the endocrine glands and their secretions in relation to their processes or functions including their care and treatment.

Levels offered: Doctoral.

Typical courses: Biochemical Methods in Endocrine Research, Polypeptide-Hormone-Receptor Interactions, Biochemistry of Steroid Hormones, Neuroendocrine Control Mechanisms, Reproductive Physiology.

Related/complementary majors: Biochemistry, Physiology.

Needed abilities: excellent aptitude for biological and chemical sciences, analytical ability.

Career possibilities: research endocrinologist.

Engineering Mechanics

Describes the theory and practical application of the action of force on bodies, with motion, and with statics, kinematics, and kinetics.

Levels offered: Bachelor's, Master's, Doctoral.

Typical courses: Stress/Strain Relations, Stability, Torsion, Inertia, Applied Elasticity.

Related/complementary majors: Engineering Physics, Engineering Science, Mechanical Engineering.

Needed abilities: excellent aptitude for mathematics and physics, analytical ability, problem-solving skills.

Career possibilities: engineer.

Engineering Physics

Describes the physical principles underlying the field of engineering.

Levels offered: Bachelor's, Master's, Doctoral.

Typical courses: Electromagnetic Theory, Analytical Mechanics and Quantum Mechanics, Thermodynamics and Statistical Mechanics, Experimental Physics.

Related/complementary majors: Engineering Science, Physics.

Needed abilities: excellent aptitude for mathematics and physics, analytical ability, problem-solving skills.

Career possibilities: engineer.

Engineering Science

Describes the usefulness of such subject matters as physics, chemistry, biology, and mathematics in engineering.

Levels offered: Bachelor's, Master's, Doctoral.

Typical courses: Engineering Thinking, Engineering Statistics, Computing for Engineering, Engineering Fluid Mechanics.

Related/complementary majors: Biophysics, Mathematics, Physical Chemistry, Physics.

Needed abilities: excellent aptitude for biology, chemistry, mathematics, and physics, analytical ability, problem-solving skills.

Career possibilities: engineer.

English Education

Describes the theories, methods, and techniques involved in teaching the subject matter of English.

Levels offered: Bachelor's, Master's, Doctoral.

Typical courses: Reading in the Secondary Schools. Great Books, Fundamental English Grammar, History of the English Language, English Curriculum in the Elementary School.

Related/complementary majors: English (General or Literature), Education (Elementary/Secondary).

Needed abilities: excellent interpersonal and communication skills, excellent aptitude for all aspects of English, analytical ability, problem-solving skills.

Career possibilities: English teacher.

English, General

Describes the skills and techniques essential to the English language.

Levels offered: Associate, Bachelor's, Master's, Doctoral.

Typical courses: Creative Writing, Speech Composition, Poetry Writing for English Majors, Modern English Grammar, English Linguistics.

Related/complementary majors: Creative Writing, English Literature, Journalism, Linguistics, Technical and Business Writing.

Needed abilities: excellent verbal aptitude (written and oral), analytical ability.

Career possibilities: copywriter, editor, writer.

Entertainment Technology

Prepares graduates to function in entry-level technical jobs in the entertainment industry.

Levels offered: Associate.

Typical courses: Lighting Technology, Sound Technology, Audiovisual Production, Television Production, Stagecraft.

Related/complementary majors: Film/Radio/Television Production, Theatre Production.

Needed abilities: aptitude for applied electronics, orientation for detail, analytical ability, problem-solving skills.

Career possibilities: light and sound technician, technical manager, performing arts production technician.

Entomology

Describes insects, including life cycle, morphology, physiology, and taxonomy.

Levels offered: Bachelor's, Master's, Doctoral.

Typical courses: Insect Genetics, Insecticide Toxicology, Insect Morphology and Evolution, Immature Insects, Insect Ecology and Pest Management.

Related/complementary majors: Biology, Horticultural Science, Plant Pathology/Protection.

Needed abilities: excellent aptitude for the biological sciences, analytical ability.

Career possibilities: researcher/scientist.

Entrepreneurship

Prepares students for the challenges of small business management and new venture creation.

Levels offered: Bachelor's, Master's.

Typical courses: Venture Initiation, Venture Growth, Entrepreneurial Finance, New Product Development, Competitive Advantage.

Related/complementary majors: Business Administration and Management, Marketing, Finance, International Business, Small Business Management and Ownership.

Needed abilities: excellent ability to envision, initiate, develop, and manage new business enterprise, risk-taking tolerance.

Career possibilities: owner/manager of a new/small business venture.

Environmental Design

Describes the processes, procedures, observations, and techniques essential to the development of designs for exterior and interior environments.

Levels offered: Bachelor's, Master's, Doctoral.

Typical courses: Design and the Natural Environment, Environment, Behavior, and Design, Environmental Design Graphics, Design and the Future, Environmental Design Theory and Methodology.

Related/complementary majors: Architecture, Interior Design, Urban Design.

Needed abilities: high degree of creativity, aptitude for applied psychology, artistic flair/good eye for color and form, problem-solving skills.

Career possibilities: environmental designer.

Environmental Engineering

Describes the engineering discipline that identifies and designs solutions to environmental problems that can impact human health and the natural world.

Levels offered: Bachelor's, Master's, Doctoral.

Typical courses: Environmental Impacts of Transportation, Environmental Organic Chemistry, Water and Wastewater Treatment, Applications of Environmental Regulations, Hazardous Waste Management.

Related/complimentary majors: Civil Engineering.

Needed abilities: excellent aptitude for mathematics and science, analytical ability, problem-solving skills.

Career possibilities: environmental engineer, manager in an environmentally-focused company.

Environmental/Occupational Health and Safety

Describes the techniques and methods to protect the workforce from illness or injury and the general public and the environment from exposure to hazardous materials.

Levels offered: Associate, Bachelor's, Master's

Typical courses: Waste Management, Environmental Regulations,

Emergency Preparedness and Training, Incident and Accident Investigation, Transportation and Storage of Hazardous Materials.

Related complementary majors: Public Health, Science.

Needed abilities: aptitude for applied science, analytical ability, problem-solving skills.

Career possibilities: occupational health and safety manager, environmental inspector.

Environmental Technology/Management

Provides the student with in-depth knowledge of environmental issues and solutions in the major environmental media (air, water, wastes).

Levels offered: Associate, Bachelor's.

Typical courses: Environmental Compliance Plans, Sampling and Analysis, Site Remediation, Environmental Permitting, Corporate Environmental Management.

Related/complementary courses: Business Management, Public Administration, Sciences.

Needed abilities: aptitude for applied science and business, analytical ability, problem-solving skills.

Career possibilities: environmental manager for industry or a public/nonprofit organization.

Epidemiology

Examines the distribution and determinants of disease frequency in human populations.

Levels offered: Master's, Doctoral.

Typical courses: Epidemiology of Cancer, Epidemiologic Analysis of Outbreaks and Infectious Diseases, Research Synthesis and Meta-Analysis, Studies in Molecular Epidemiology.

Related/complementary majors: Biology, Biostatistics, Computer Science, Psychology, Public Health, Sociology.

Career possibilities: researcher, public health analyst.

Equestrian Studies

Prepares individuals to ride horses and perform related duties.

Levels offered: Associate, Bachelor's (limited number of programs).

Typical courses: Equine Judging and Evaluation, Breeding and Management, Theory of Teaching Equitation, Grooming and Showing, basic Horsemanship.

Related/complementary majors: Animal Science.

Needed abilities: aptitude for biological science and business as applied to horses, aptitude for riding/judging/showing horses.

Career possibilities: equestrian judge, riding instructor.

Equine Science/Business Management

Prepares individuals to work in the horse industry (training, care, business).

Levels offered: Associate, Bachelor's.

Typical courses: Horse Evaluation, Horse Production and Management, Horse Nutrition, Horse Equipment and Facilities, Fundamentals of Horse Handling and Training.

Related/complementary courses: Animal Science, Business Management.

Needed abilities: aptitude for applied business and science.

Career possibilities: horse breeder, trainer, sales representative for equine products.

Exercise Physiology/Science

Deals with the study of immediate and short-term effects of physical activity on the human body.

Levels offered: Bachelor's, Master's, Doctoral.

Typical courses: Exercise Programming for Older Adults, Exercise Testing, Cardiovascular Physiology, Fitness Assessment and Exercise Prescription, Exercise Physiology Lab.

Related/complementary majors: Physical Therapy, Sports Medicine, Physiology.

Needed abilities: excellent aptitude for biological science, analytical ability, problem-solving skills, good interpersonal skills.

Career possibilities: coach, fitness instructor, exercise physiologist.

Experimental Psychology

Describes the general body of methods, data, and laws that have been derived by scientific research, including theoretical and systematic points of view applicable to the prediction, control, and understanding of the behavior of individual human organisms and other species.

Levels offered: Master's, Doctoral.

Typical courses: Learning and Motivation Laboratory, Modification of Sensory Systems, Seminar on Visual Information Processing, Methods and Topics in Experimental Social psychology, Experimental Analysis.

Related/complementary majors: Cognitive Psychology, Psychometrics, Quantitative Psychology, Statistics.

Needed abilities: excellent aptitude for psychological science, good aptitude for statistics, analytical ability.

Career possibilities: research laboratory psychologist.

Family and Community Services

Provides students with the understanding and skills to assist families and provide support services to the community.

Levels offered: Associate, Bachelor's.

Typical courses: Parent Education, Family Development, Preschool Guidance, One-parent Family, Human Sexuality.

Related/complementary majors: Human Development and Family Studies, Sociology.

Needed abilities: excellent aptitude for psychosocial science, analytical ability, problem-solving skills, excellent communication skills.

Career possibilities: counselor, family issues writer, human services worker.

Family and Consumer Science Education

Describes the theories, methods, and techniques of designing, implementing, and evaluating programs which prepare, upgrade, and retrain students for homemaking and wage-earning occupations requiring the knowledge of skills of home economics subject matter.

Levels offered: Bachelor's, Master's, Doctoral.

Typical courses: Food and People, Clothing, Textiles, and the Human Environment, Housing and Interiors, Consumer Education, Perspectives in Family and Consumer Education.

Related/complementary majors: Education, Food Science and Nutrition, Interior Design, Textiles and Clothing, Family Resource Management and Consumer Sciences.

Career possibilities: family and consumer science teacher.

Family Resource Management and Consumer Sciences

Describes the concepts, skills, and processes through which decisions about the use of resources are directed towards goal achievement in home and family living.

Levels offered: Bachelor's, Master's.

Typical courses: Communication in Human and Family Development, Linking Families and Communities, Economics of Aging, Family Financial Counseling, Consumer Behavior.

Related/complementary majors: Individual and Family Development, Family and Community Services.

Needed abilities: aptitude for applied psychosocial science, aptitude for applied economics, analytical ability, problem-solving skills, excellent communication skills.

Career possibilities: consumer rights advocate, credit counselor.

Fashion Design

Describes the design and production of garments and accessories.

Levels offered: Associate, Bachelor's, Master's (limited number of programs).

Typical courses: Garment Construction, Tailoring, Draping, Patternmaking, Fashion Illustration.

Related/complementary majors: Fashion Merchandising, Textiles and Clothing.

Needed abilities: artistic ability, creativity, flair for fashion.

Career possibilities: costume designer for theater or film, fashion designer, fashion illustrator.

Fashion Merchandising

Prepares individuals to engage in the marketing of apparel and accessories, with particular emphasis given to fashion selling and buying, fashion cycles, fashion coordination, and specialized consulting services.

Levels offered: Associate, Bachelor's, limited number of Master's and Doctoral.

Typical courses: Display and Visual Merchandising, Merchandising Mathematics, Consumer Buying, Principles of Retailing, Fashion Promotion.

Related/complementary majors: Fashion Design, Advertising, Marketing, Retailing, Textiles and Clothing.

Needed abilities: good eye for and understanding of fashion, analytical ability, problem-solving skills, creativity, good interpersonal skills, managerial aptitude.

Career possibilities: buyer, display coordinator, retail or wholesale fashion manager.

Fiber/Textiles/Weaving

Develops skills working with fibrous materials (threads, yarns, etc.) to form fabrics, materials, or art pieces.

Levels offered: Bachelor's, Master's.

Typical courses: Off-Loom Weaving, Batik, Tapestry, Dye Theory and Application.

Related/complementary majors: Art History and Appreciation, Fashion Design, Textiles and Clothing.

Needed abilities: eye for artistic detail, creativity, manual dexterity.

Career possibilities: textile artist, textile designer.

Film Studies

Describes the historic development, aesthetic qualities, theories, techniques, and creative processes of the moving image as a means of artistic expression using film as the medium.

Levels offered: Bachelor's, Master's, Doctoral (limited number of programs).

Typical courses: Film Genres, Advanced Film Script Analysis, Film Style Analysis, Seminar in Film Criticism, Basic Dramatic Screenwriting.

Related/complementary majors: Drama, Video.

Needed abilities: eye for visual details, analytical ability.

Career possibilities: film critic, film librarian, movie director/producer/screenwriter.

Finance

Prepares individuals to plan, manage, and analyze financial and monetary aspects and performance of business enterprises, banking institutions, and other organizations.

Levels offered: Bachelor's, Master's, Doctoral.

Typical courses: Real Estate Equity Valuation, Short-Term Financial Management, Risk Management, Advanced Portfolio Theory and Practice, Merger's and Acquisition.

Related/complementary majors: Banking, Business Administration and Management, Economics, Investments and Securities, Real Estate.

Needed abilities: excellent aptitude for business, analytical ability.

Career possibilities: financial analyst, financial manager.

Fine Arts

Describes the historic development, aesthetic qualities, and creative processes of two or more of the fine arts.

Levels offered: Associate, Bachelor's.

Typical courses: Watercolor Painting, Art of the Renaissance, Sculpture, Figure Drawing.

Related/complementary majors: Art History and Appreciation, Drawing, Painting, Sculpture.

Needed abilities: artistic talent, creativity.

Career possibilities: artist, art teacher.

Fire Science and Technology

Prepares individuals to function as a fire control and prevention professional.

Levels offered: Associate, Bachelor's.

Typical courses: Fire Prevention and Inspection, Fireground Hydraulics, Fire Protection Systems, Fire Apparatus and Water Supply, Rescue Operations.

Related/complementary majors: Emergency Medical Technology, Environmental/Occupational Health and Safety Technology.

Needed abilities: ability to understand applied physics and chemistry, analytical ability, problem-solving skills, ability to utilize good judgment and cope in emergency situations.

Career possibilities: firefighter, fire prevention educator.

Fire Service Administration

Describes the theories, principles, and techniques of developing, administering, and managing services for fire protection, firefighting, and rescue.

Levels offered: Bachelor's, Master's.

Typical courses: Fire Investigations, Fires Science Law, Fire Department Organization and Administration, Fiscal Management in Fire Protection, Emergency Service Delivery.

Related/complementary majors: Public Administration.

Needed abilities: managerial ability, analytical ability, problem-solving skills, aptitude for applied chemistry and physics.

Career possibilities: fire department administrator.

Fishing and Fisheries

Prepares individuals to engage in fishing for commercial purposes, and to apply the physical and biological principles and practices that promote the understanding and management of fish resources to optimize production in fresh and salt waters.

Levels offered: Associate, Bachelor's, Master's.

Typical courses: Catfish Production, Fish Genetics and Breeding, Fish Nutrition, Commercial Marine Fisheries, Commercial Marine Fisheries, Crustacean and Molluscan Aquaculture.

Related/complementary majors: Food Sciences, Agricultural Business/Production.

Needed abilities: aptitude for biological and physical sciences, analytical ability, problem-solving skills.

Career possibilities: fisheries manager.

Folklore and Mythology

Describes the role that traditions in music, art, dance, literature, and speech play in human development and cultural existence.

Levels offered: Bachelor's, Master's, Doctoral.

Typical courses: The Literature of Myth and Oral Tradition, Folk Speech, The Ballad, Folklore in Urban Environments, African-American Folklore and Culture.

Related/complementary majors: Art History and Appreciation, Comparative Literature, History, Music History and Appreciation, Sociology, Ethic Studies such as African-American Studies.

Needed abilities: aptitude for social science, understanding and appreciation of art, music, and literature, analytical ability.

Career possibilities: museum worker, teacher, performer such as a storyteller.

Food Engineering

Describes the study of food and food components as engineering materials used to produce, preserve, process, and distribute foods.

Levels offered: Bachelor's, Master's, Doctoral.

Typical courses: Food Engineering Analysis, Kinetics, Food, and Biological Systems, Physical Properties of Biological Materials, Food Machine Design.

Related/complementary majors: Biophysics, Food Science.

Needed abilities: excellent aptitude for physics, biology, and mathematics, analytical ability, problem-solving skills.

Career possibilities: food engineer, food production manager.

Food Sciences

Describes the principles and practices involved in converting agricultural products to forms suitable for direct human consumption or for storage.

Levels offered: Associate, Bachelor's, Master's, Doctoral.

Typical courses: Food Microbiology, Food Analysis and Quality Control, Food Plant Sanitation, Meat Selection and Grading, Industrial Food Preservation Technology.

Related/complementary majors: Agricultural Production, Food Engineering.

Needed abilities: excellent aptitude for biological and chemical sciences, analytical ability, problem-solving skills.

Career possibilities: food technologist, distribution specialist, researcher.

Foreign Languages

Describes the structure and use of language that is common or indigenous to people of the same community or nation, the same geographical area, or the same cultural traditions. May include: * African (Non-Semitic) Languages, such as Ibo, Swahili, Yoruba. * Asiatic Languages, such as Chinese, Japanese, Korean. * Balto-Slavic Languages, such as Latvian, Lettish, Russian, Polish, Czech, Serbo-Croatian, Ukrainian. * Germanic Languages, such as German, Scandinavian (Norwegian, Swedish, Danish), Yiddish. * Indic Languages, such as Hindi, Sanskrit, Urdu, Bengali, Punjabi. * Greek (Classical and Modern) Languages. Italic Languages, such as French, Latin, Portuguese, Spanish. Semitic Languages, such as Arabic and Hebrew.

Levels offered: Associate, Bachelor's, Master's, Doctoral.

Typical courses: Germanic Civilization and Culture, History of the Spanish Language, Survey of French Literature, Conversational Japanese.

Relate/complementary majors: Area and Ethnic Studies, Comparative Literature, Linguistics, International Business.

Needed abilities: excellent ear for all aspects of a foreign language, excellent oral and written communication skills.

Career possibilities: interpreter/translator, diplomatic worker, international businessperson.

Foreign Languages Education

Describes the theories, methods, and techniques involved in teaching the subject matter of foreign languages.

Levels offered: Bachelor's, Master's, Doctoral.

Typical courses: Applied Linguistics, Teaching Foreign Language to Elementary Students, French Conversation and Composition, German Grammar and Structure.

Related/complementary majors: Education, Foreign Languages.

Needed abilities: excellent interpersonal and communication skills, excellent aptitude for one or more foreign languages.

Career possibilities: foreign language teacher.

Forensic Science/Studies

Combines physical science, the law, and criminal investigation to enable the evidentiary process of the criminal justice system, from the investigation and collection of crime scene evidence to its scientific evaluation and subsequent presentation in court.

Levels offered: Associate, Bachelor's, Master's.

Typical courses: Law and Evidence, Hair and Fiber Morphology, Quantitative Analysis, Forensic Examination of Paints and Pigments, Toxicology.

Related/complementary majors: Chemistry, Physics, Criminal Justice.

Needed abilities: excellent aptitude for biological and chemical science, analytical ability, problem-solving skills, ability to apply legal principles, orientation to details, ability to work precisely according to established standards.

Career possibilities: forensic scientist/technician.

Forestry

Prepares individuals to apply the science, art, and practice of managing and using for human benefit the natural resources that occur on and in association with forest lands.

Levels offered: Associate, Bachelor's, Master's, Doctoral.

Typical courses: Trees Physiology, Recreational Use of Forest and Parks, Urban Forestry, Forest Pathology and Protection.

Related/complementary majors: Conservation Biology, Horticulture, Soil Science.

Needed abilities: aptitude for biological science, analytical ability, problem-solving skills.

Career possibilities: forest ranger/administrator.

Forestry Production and Processing

Prepares individuals to produce, protect, and manage timber and specialty forest crops; maintain, operate and repair related

71

equipment and machinery; harvest and transport trees as a crop; and select, grade, and market forest raw materials for converting into a variety of consumer goods.

Levels offered: Associate, Bachelor's, Master's, Doctoral.

Typical courses: Pulp and Paper Technology, Adhesive Bonding of Wood Composites, Wood Identification and Products, Physics of Wood and Wood Composites, Deterioration and Wood Treating Processes.

Related/complementary majors: Agricultural majors.

Needed abilities: aptitude for applied physical science, aptitude for business.

Career possibilities: lumber industry manager, lumber salesperson.

Gaming/Casino Management

Trains individuals to operate casinos and other gaming establishments.

Levels offered: Bachelor's.

Typical courses: Gaming Device, Casino Operations, Casino Accounting, Gaming Internship, Casino Products, Protection, and Probability.

Related/complementary majors: Hotel Management.

Needed abilities: aptitude for business, analytical ability, problem-solving skills, managerial ability.

Career possibilities: casino manager/supervisor.

Genetics

Describes the inheritance of traits and character in human beings and animals.

Levels offered: Bachelor's, Master's, Doctoral.

Typical courses: Genetic Engineering, Human Heredity and Society, Genetic Statistics, Advanced Molecular Genetics.

Related/complementary majors: Biology, Zoology, Statistics.

Needed abilities: excellent aptitude for biology and statistics, analytical ability.

Career possibilities: genetics researcher, genetics counselor.

Geochemistry

Describes the chemical composition, structure, and reaction of earth materials.

Levels offered: Master's, Doctoral.

Typical courses: Phase Diagrams, Chemical Thermodynamics, Geologic Problems, Chemical Aspects of Igneous Metamorphic and Sedimentary Rocks.

Related/complementary majors: Physical Chemistry, Geology, Geophysics and Seismology.

Needed abilities: excellent aptitude for the physical and chemical sciences, analytical ability.

Career possibilities: energy company consultant/researcher.

Geography

Describes the earth and its life (land, sea, and air) and distribution of plant and animal life, including human beings and industries.

Levels offered: Associate, Bachelor's, Master's, Doctoral.

Typical courses: Human Geography, Geography of Food, Map Interpretation, World Regional Geography, Human Impact Upon Environment.

Related/complementary majors: Urban and Regional Planning, Surveying and Mapping Sciences.

Needed abilities: understanding of natural resources, analytical ability.

Career possibilities: cartographer, regional/urban/community planner, researcher for private agencies or government industries.

Geological/Geophysical Engineering

Describes the practical application of scientific principles related to the physical history of the earth, the rocks and soils of which it is composed, and the physical changes in its structure.

Levels offered: Bachelor's, Master's, Doctoral.

Typical courses: Rock Mechanics, Sedimentology, Mine Survey, Mineralogy, Rock Engineering.

Related/complementary majors: Geochemistry, Geology.

Needed abilities: excellent aptitude for physics and mathematics, analytical ability, problem-solving skills.

Career possibilities: geological engineer.

Geology

Describes the earth and other celestial bodies, including their composition, structure, history, and related changes.

Levels offered: Bachelor's, Master's, Doctoral.

Typical courses: Clay Mineralogy, Plutonic Rocks, Marine Geology, Stratigraphy, Mineral Deposits.

Related/complementary majors: Earth Science, Geochemistry, Geophysics and Seismology, Planetary Science.

Needed abilities: aptitude for physical science, analytical ability.

Career possibilities: energy company or government researcher/consultant.

Geophysics and Seismology

Describes the effects of physical phenomena on the earth, and earthquakes and artificially produced vibrations in the earth.

Levels offered: Bachelor's, Master's, Doctoral.

Typical courses: Gravity and Magnetic Methods of Exploration, Global Geophysics and Geodynamics, Linear System and Signal Analysis, Introduction to Tectonophysics and Elastic Waves.

Related/complementary majors: Earth Science, Geology, Physics.

Needed abilities: excellent aptitude for physical science, analytical ability.

Career possibilities: energy company researcher/consultant, seismologist.

Gerontology

Describes the aging process and the techniques to help older adults.

Levels offered: Associate, Bachelor's, Master's, Doctoral.

Typical courses: Historical Perspectives of Aging, Aging in American Society, Physiology of Aging, Recreation for the Elderly, Death, Loss and Grief.

Related/complementary majors: Psychology, Sociology, Occupational Therapy, Physical Therapy, Recreation, Recreational Therapy, Music Therapy, Art Therapy, Adult and Continuing Education, Nutrition, Health Care Administration.

Needed abilities: aptitude for psychosocial science, analytical ability, problem-solving skills, good interpersonal skills.

Career possibilities: gerontologist/researcher, provider/administrator/policy maker of recreational, educational, nutritional, social, and other services to the aged.

Glass

Develops skills in forming or shaping a mass of molten or heat-softened glass into functional and decorative items.

Levels offered: Bachelor's, Master's.

Typical courses: Glass Blowing, Acid Etching, Flat Glass Techniques, Engraving, Polishing.

Related/complementary courses: Art History and Appreciation, Fine Arts.

Needed abilities: eye for artistic detail (form and color), excellent manual dexterity, creativity.

Career possibilities: glass artist.

Graphic Design

Describes the theories, aesthetic qualities, and creative processes for effective communication of ideas, information, and feelings in printed form.

Levels offered: Associate, Bachelor's, Master's.

Typical courses: Art Direction, Editorial Illustration, Advertising Illustration, Introduction to Typography, Advanced Graphic Design.

Related/complementary majors: Advertising, Illustration Design, Photography.

Needed abilities: aptitude for applied psychology and communication, eye for artistic detail, creativity.

Career possibilities: advertising artist, art editor/director, graphic designer.

Graphic Technology

Describes the use of hot- , cold-, or computer typesetting, including layout, composition, press work, binding, lithography, photo-engraving, and other graphic arts relating to the printing industry.

Levels offered: Associate, Bachelor's (limited number of programs).

Typical courses: Photo Typesetting, Binding and Finishing Process, Color Theory and Practice, Offset Photography Stripping and Platemaking, Estimating of Printing and Materials.

Related/complementary majors: Photography, Graphic Design.

Needed abilities: eye for artistic detail, good manual dexterity, good visual perception, problem-solving skills, ability to work according to precise standards.

Career possibilities: graphic arts/printing technician.

Health Care Administration

Describes the principles and procedures of planning, organizing, and controlling health care facilities and programs.

Levels offered: Bachelor's, Master's, Doctoral.

Typical courses: Health Care Organization and Services, Personnel Management in Health Care Facilities, Health Planning and Political Process, Health Economics, Management in Health Care Facilities.

Related/complementary majors: Business Administration, Public Administration.

Needed abilities: aptitude for business, analytical ability, problem-solving skills, managerial skills.

Career possibilities: hospital administrator, health acre agency director.

Health Education

Describes the theories, methods, and techniques in teaching the subject matter of health education.

Levels offered: Bachelor's, Master's, Doctoral.

Typical courses: Human Nutrition, Human Sexuality, Drug Education, Safety Education, School and Community Health Resources.

Related/complementary majors: Education, Food Science and Nutrition, Nursing, Physical Education, Public Health.

Needed abilities: excellent interpersonal and communication skills, analytical ability, problem-solving skills, aptitude for biological science.

Career possibilities: drug educator, health educator.

Health Information Management

Prepares individuals to process, analyze, validate, and distribute health care information.

Levels offered: Associate, Bachelor's, Master's.

Typical courses: Information Technology in Heath Systems, Data Base Management in Health Care, Medical Terminology, Legal Aspects of Health Information, Procedural Coding.

Related/complementary majors: Information Sciences, Medical Office Technology, Epidemiology.

Needed abilities: analytical ability, orientation to details, computer aptitude.

Career possibilities: health information administrator or technician.

Higher Education Administration

Describes the principles and techniques of planning, organizing, developing, staffing, coordinating, managing, researching, evaluating, financing, and controlling higher education institutions and agencies.

Levels offered: Master's, Doctoral.

Typical courses: Higher Education in the United States, College Personnel Policies and Practices, Student Development in Higher Education, Planning Facilities for Higher Education.

Related/complementary majors: Adult and Continuing Education Administration, Community College Administration.

Needed abilities: ability to coordinate educational theory and practices with management principles, analytical ability, problem-solving skills.

Career possibilities: college or university administrator.

Historic Preservation

Describes the techniques and processes for protecting historical sites and buildings from deterioration and decay, and for restoring these buildings.

Levels offered: Master's, Doctoral.

Typical courses: American Preservation Policy and Practice, Historic Site Curatorship, Preservation Building Trade Techniques, Architectural Pathology, History of American Architecture.

Related/complementary majors: Architecture, History, Environmental Design, Urban Design.

Needed abilities: aptitude for history and architecture, eye for visual detail, analytical ability, problem-solving skills.

Career possibilities: curator, historic renovator.

History

Describes the past, including the recording, gathering, criticizing, synthesizing, and interpreting evidence about past facts.

Levels offered: Associate, Bachelor's, Master's, Doctoral.

Typical courses: Medieval Britain, The American West, History of Western Civilization, Ancient Egypt, The Second World War.

Related/complementary majors: Area and Ethnic Studies, Medieval and Renaissance Studies, Political Science and Government, African-American Studies, Women's Studies.

Needed abilities: aptitude for social science, analytical ability.

Career possibilities: archival and museum worker, historical researcher.

Horticultural Science

Describes the principles and practices involved in the production of fruits and vegetables and the management of the pests of these crops.

Levels offered: Associate, Bachelor's, Master's, Doctoral.

Typical courses: Fruit and Nut Culture, Breeding of Horticulture Crops, Orchard Management, Fruit and Vegetable Production, Physiology of Horticultural Products Following Harvest.

Related/complementary majors: Agronomy, Agriculture, Botany, Entomology, Plant Physiology, Plant Protection.

Needed abilities: excellent aptitude for biological science, analytical ability, problem-solving skills.

Career possibilities: orchard or vegetable farm manager, researcher.

Horticulture

Prepares individuals to produce, process, and market plants, shrubs, and trees and to establish, maintain, and manager horticultural enterprises.

Levels offered: Associate, Bachelor's, Master's, Doctoral.

Typical courses: Floriculture, Herbaceous Ornamental Plants, Greenhouse Management, Formulation and Application of Pesticides, Tropical Plants.

Related/complementary majors: Business, Plant Sciences.

Needed abilities: aptitude for business and biology, analytical ability, problem-solving skills.

Career possibilities: greenhouse or nursery manager, landscaper, researcher.

Hotel/Motel/Restaurant/Institutional Management

Describes the nature and application of management methods to hotels, motels, restaurants, and other institutions related to hospitality.

Levels offered: Associate, Bachelor's, Master's, Doctoral.

Typical courses: Food and Beverage Management, Business and Hospitality Law, Marketing for Hotels and Restaurants, Environmental Service Management, Fundamentals of Hospitality Supervision.

Related/complementary majors: Business Administration and Management, Small Business Administration/Entrepreneurship.

Needed abilities: aptitude for all aspects of business, managerial ability, good interpersonal skills, analytical ability, problem-solving skills.

Career possibilities: hotel/motel/restaurant manager (front desk, food and beverage, housekeeping, sales, general).

Human Development and Family Studies

Describes the basic development and behavioral characteristics of the individual within the context of the family from conception through death.

Levels offered: Associate, Bachelor's, Master's, Doctoral.

Typical courses: Marriage and Family Relations, Infancy, Directing Behavior and Development of Children, Family Intervention Models, Masculine-Feminine Roles.

Related/complementary majors: Family and Community Services, Developmental Psychology, Sociology.

Needed abilities: excellent aptitude for psychosocial science, analytical ability, problem-solving skills, excellent interpersonal skills.

Career possibilities: human services, writer on child development and family relations.

Human Resources Management

Describes the methods, principles, procedures, and theories necessary to manage people within the workplace.

Levels offered: Bachelor's, Master's, Doctoral.

Typical courses: Legal Issues in Personnel, Compensation Administration, Contract Negotiation and Administration, Managing Diversity, Benefits Analysis.

Related/complementary majors: Business Administration/Management, Industrial and Organizational Psychology, Law.

Needed abilities: aptitude for applied psychology, business and law, analytical ability, problem-solving skills, good interpersonal skills.

Career possibilities: personnel manager, recruiter, benefits manager.

Human Services

Prepares students to work in human services in public/private nonprofit programs.

Levels offered: Associate, Bachelor's.

Typical courses: Child Welfare, Crisis Intervention, Working with Families, Interviewing Skills, Human Services Program Development and Evaluation.

Related/complementary majors: Psychology, Sociology, Family and Community Services, Social Work.

Needed abilities: aptitude for applied psychology and sociology, analytical ability, problem-solving skills, excellent interpersonal skills.

Career possibilities: human service worker.

Humanities

Describes the study of historical figures, creative works of art and literature, systems of philosophy, and religious traditions that are the common property of educated people.

Levels offered: Associate, Bachelor's, Master's, Doctoral.

Typical courses: Idealism and Existentialism, Platonic Ideal, Shakespeare, Renaissance and Reformation, Literary Criticism.

Related/complementary majors: Literature, Art History and Appreciation, Classics, Folklore and Mythology, History, Philosophy, Religion, Renaissance and Medieval Studies.

Needed abilities: aptitude for literature, art, history, philosophy, and religion, analytical ability.

Career possibilities: teacher, writer.

Illustration

Describes the techniques for conveying information through visual imagery and pictorial representation.

Levels offered: Associate, Bachelor's, Master's.

Typical courses: Situational Figure Drawing, Rendering, Cartooning. Beginning Anatomy, Elements of Design.

Related/complementary majors: Drawing, Painting.

Needed abilities: excellent artistic ability, creativity.

Career possibilities: illustrator.

Industrial and Organizational Psychology

Describes the application of psychological knowledge and methodology to specific work-related problems in industry and government.

Levels offered: Master's, Doctoral.

Typical courses: Power and Politics in Organizations, Negotiation, Managing Groups in Organizations, Laboratory Experimentation with Organizations, Management of Organizational Change.

Related/complementary majors: Social Psychology, Business Administration and Management, Human Resources Management.

Needed abilities: excellent aptitude for psychological and social sciences, some ability to understand business practices, analytical ability, problem-solving skills.

Career possibilities: industrial/organizational psychologist.

Industrial Design

Describes the techniques of designing consumer or commercial products and packaging to minimize aesthetic appeal and maximizing utilitarian aspects.

Levels offered: Bachelor's, Master's.

Typical courses: Product Design, Presentation Methods, Transportation Design, Advanced Comprehensive Design.

Related/complementary majors: aptitude for applied psychology, eye for artistic detail, analytical ability, problem-solving skills.

Career possibilities: package designer, product designer.

Industrial Engineering

Describes the organization and management of integrated systems of management of people, materials, and equipment for the purpose of improving production processes.

Levels offered: Bachelor's, Master's, Doctoral.

Typical courses: Modeling and Analysis of Large Scale Systems, Computer Applications in Industry, Reliability Engineering, Industrial Safety, Engineering Economics for Management.

Related/complementary majors: Business Administration and Management.

Needed abilities: excellent aptitude for physics and mathematics, analytical ability, problem-solving skills.

Career possibilities: industrial engineer/manager.

Industrial Technology

Describes the design and installation of integrated systems of materials, equipment, and personnel for manufacturing.

Levels offered: Associate, Bachelor's.

Typical courses: Safety Programs, Hydraulic Controls, Product manufacture, Engineering Drawing, Metal Fabrication.

Related/complementary majors: Drafting and Design Technology, Manufacturing Technology, Mechanical Design Technology, Quality Control Technology.

Needed abilities: aptitude for physical science and mathematics, analytical ability, problem-solving skills.

Career possibilities: production manager, quality control technician.

Information Science and Management/Systems

Describes the application of information technology to organizational and managerial needs.

Levels offered: Bachelor's, Master's, Doctoral.

Typical courses: Systems Analysis and Design, Applied Database Management, Organizational Informatics, Information Architecture and Design, Introduction to Research and Statistics.

Related/complementary majors: Business Management, Computer Science, Library Science.

Needed abilities: aptitude for technology and business, analytical skills, problem-solving skills.

Career possibilities: manager, systems analyst.

Inorganic Chemistry

Describes all the elements and their compounds, including the isolation, compositions, structures, physical and spectroscopic properties, syntheses, energy relationships, and chemical transformations of these substances, but excluding the hydrocarbons and most of their derivatives.

Levels offered: Master's, Doctoral.

Typical courses: Acid-Base Chemistry, Differential Analysis, Coordination Chemistry of the Transitional Elements, Radiochemistry, Atomic Structure.

Related/complementary majors: General Chemistry.

Needed abilities: excellent aptitude for chemical science, analytical ability.

Career possibilities: chemist.

Instrumentation Technology

Prepares individuals to design, develop, test, and evaluate control or measurement devices.

Levels offered: Associate, Bachelor's.

Typical courses: Measurement Systems Analysis, Process and Instrument Diagrams, Electronic and Electrical Systems in Instrumentation, Pressure/Level/Flow Measurement and Control, Temperature Measurement and Control.

Related/complementary majors: Electrical/Electronic Technology.

Needed abilities: good aptitude for applied physics, analytical ability, problem-solving skills, orientation to detail.

Career possibilities: instrumentation technician.

Insurance and Risk Management

Describes risk analysis and personal and business insurance and their applications to health, life, disability, property, liability, and fiduciary trust and annuity underwriting.

Levels offered: Associate, Bachelor's, Master's, Doctoral.

Typical courses: Health Insurance, Estate Planning, Property and Casualty Insurance, Risk Management, Life Insurance.

Related/complementary courses: Actuarial Sciences, Investments and Securities.

Needed abilities: strong aptitude for business and mathematics, analytical ability, orientation to details.

Career possibilities: insurance analyst, insurance sales representative, insurance underwriter.

Interior Design

Describes the processes, procedures, observations, and techniques essential to the development of designs for interior environments.

Levels offered: Associate, Bachelor's, Master's.

Typical courses: Spatial Design, Computer-Aided Residential Design, Interior Plantscape, Interior Environmental Design, Residential Lighting.

Related/complementary majors: Environmental Design, Art.

Needed abilities: excellent aptitude for artistic detail such as color and line, creativity, problem-solving skills, good understanding of applied psychology.

Career possibilities: interior designer, designer of home furnishings, home furnishings sales representatives.

International Agriculture

Prepares individuals to apply the social, biological, and agricultural sciences and technologies as they relate to food production and distribution on a worldwide level.

Levels offered: Bachelor's, Master's, Doctoral.

Typical courses: World and United States Agricultural Trade, Economics of Agriculture, Agricultural Cooperatives, Statistical Analysis of Agriculture, Distribution and Marketing of Agricultural Products.

Related/complementary majors: Agricultural Economics, Area and Ethnic Studies, International Business Management.

Needed abilities: aptitude for business principles and agricultural practices, analytical ability, problem-solving skills.

Career possibilities: commodities analyst/futures trader, marketing representative for an international agricultural products firm, Peace Corps worker.

International and Comparative Education

Describes the difference between educational theory and practice in different countries and various cultures for the purpose of deepening understanding and solving of educational problems.

Levels offered: Master's, Doctoral.

Typical courses: Asian Education and Cultural Change, Education and the Development of nations, Role of Research and Evaluation in International Education, Educational Planning in International Education Development.

Related/complementary majors: Anthropology, Area and Ethic Studies, Sociology.

Needed abilities: aptitude for educational theory and social sciences, analytical ability, problem-solving skills.

Career possibilities: educational analyst or consultant.

85

International Business Management

Describes the principles and processes of export sales, trade controls, foreign operations, monetary problems, and other areas of concern in the international business environment as it affects, or is affected by, a company's policies, procedures, and products.

Levels offered: Bachelor's, Master's, Doctoral.

Typical courses: International marketing, Comparative Economic Systems, International Transportation, Management of Multinational Firms, Cultural Dimensions of International Business.

Related/complementary majors: Area and Ethic Studies, Business and Management, Economics, International Studies.

Needed abilities: ability to understand and apply complex business principles, analytical ability, problem-solving skills.

Career possibilities: business person on an international level.

International Studies

Provides an interdisciplinary approach to understanding countries around the world and their interaction with each other.

Levels offered: Bachelor's, Master's, Doctoral.

Typical courses: Ethics, Religion, and International Politics, International Social Justice, International Economics, Language and Culture, Comparative Politics.

Related/complementary majors: Anthropology, International Business Management, Area and Ethic Studies, Economics, Geography, History, Political Science and Government, Sociology, Humanities.

Needed abilities: excellent aptitude for all the social sciences, strong analytical ability, problem-solving skills; may require fluency in a foreign language.

Career possibilities: diplomat, business executive, policy analyst, government worker on the international level.

Investments and Securities

Describes the securities market, investment concepts, and the effects of economic business cycles on investments.

Levels offered: Bachelor's, Master's, Doctoral.

Typical courses: International Finance, Securities Analysis, Corporate Finance, Portfolio Theory and Management.
Related/complementary majors: Economics.
Needed abilities: aptitude for economics, analytical ability.
Career possibilities: financial planner, investment analyst, portfolio manager, securities representative.

Jazz and Improvisation

Prepares students to understand the history of and perform jazz.
Levels offered: Bachelor's, Master's, Doctoral.
Typical courses: Analytical History of Jazz, Jazz Piano, Jazz Arranging, Jazz Composition, Jazz Improvisation.
Related/complementary majors: Music History, Music Performance.
Needed abilities: ability to appreciate and perform jazz.
Career possibilities: jazz performer/teacher.

Jewish Studies

Describes the history, society, politics, culture, and economics of the Jewish people.
Levels offered: Bachelor's, master's, Doctoral.
Typical courses: Jewish Ethics and Values, Modern Jewish Civilization, Humanity and Jewish Identity, Israel as Idea and State, Topics in Jewish Literature.
Related/complementary majors: Anthropology, Art History and Appreciation, Comparative Literature, History, Music History and Appreciation, Psychology, Religion, Sociology.
Needed abilities: aptitude for all aspects of the social sciences and humanities, analytical ability.
Career possibilities: program director of Jewish cultural center, writer of Jewish topics.

Journalism

Describes the principles and methods of gathering, processing, evaluating, and disseminating through mass media, information about current events and issues.
Levels offered: Associate, Bachelor's, Master's, Doctoral.

Typical courses: Magazine Writing and Editing, Newswriting, Journalism Ethics, Photojournalism, The Press in Contemporary Society.

Related/complementary majors: Communications, English, Photography, Radio/Television.

Needed abilities: excellent oral/written communication skills, analytical ability, orientation to detail.

Career possibilities: journalist, writer.

Kinesiology

Trains individuals to help others enhance the quality of their lives through physical activity.

Levels offered: Bachelor's, Master's, Doctoral.

Typical courses: Movement for Relaxation and Revitalization, Biomechanics, Therapeutic Exercise, Motor Control, Coordination, and Skill, Fitness Evaluation and Exercise Prescription.

Related/complementary majors: Exercise Physiology, Sports Medicine, Physical Therapy, Physical Education.

Needed abilities: aptitude for biology, analytical ability, good interpersonal skills.

Career possibilities: fitness instructor, wellness facilitator, athletic director, personal trainer.

Labor/Industrial Relations

Describes the study of work and the employment relationship, including areas of federal and state legislation, union contracts, labor negotiation, conciliation, arbitration, and grievance procedures.

Levels offered: Bachelor's, Master's, Doctoral.

Typical courses: Labor Union Administration, Economics of Wages and Employment, Collective Bargaining, Labor Relations Law and Legislation, Competition, and Conflict Resolution.

Related/complementary majors: Conflict Resolution, Industrial and Organizational Psychology, law, Organizational Behavior, Human Resources.

Needed abilities: aptitude for business and social science, analytical ability, problem-solving skills, good interpersonal skills.

Career possibilities: collective bargainer/arbitrator, personnel manager, union worker.

Landscape Architecture

Describes the design processes as applied to manmade structures and objects and animate and inanimate natural materials in the landscape with the object of furthering human knowledge of functional relationships, human behavior, ecology, land form, construction technology and aesthetic sensitivity.

Levels offered: Bachelor's, Master's, Doctoral.

Typical courses: Landscape Resource Management, Plant Materials and Planting Design, Landscape Establishment and Maintenance, Ecology in Landscape Planning, Site Construction and Structures.

Related/complementary courses: Environmental Design, Horticulture.

Needed abilities: good eye for artistic detail, aptitude for horticulture, analytical ability, problem-solving skills and creativity.

Career possibilities: environmental planner, landscape architect.

Laser Electro-Optic Technology

Prepares individuals to assist engineers, scientists, or industrial managers in the assembly, installation, testing, adjustment, and operation of various types of lasers.

Levels offered: Associate.

Typical courses: Optical Electronics, Fundamentals of Quantum Mechanics, Digital Image Processing, Fiber Optics, Electro Magnetics.

Related/complementary majors: Electronic Technology.

Needed abilities: good aptitude for applied physical science and mathematics, analytical ability, problem-solving skills, mechanical aptitude.

Career possibilities: laser technician.

Latin American Studies

Describes the history, society, politics, culture, and economics of Latin America.

Levels offered: Bachelor's, Master's, Doctoral.

Typical courses: History of Mexico and Central America, Trends and Figures in Literature of Spanish America, Brazilian Culture, Latin American Ethnology, The United States and Latin America.

Related/complementary majors: Anthropology, Art History and Appreciation, Comparative Literature, Economics, International Studies, International Business management, Music History and Appreciation, Political Science and Government, Sociology, Spanish.

Needed abilities: excellent aptitude for all aspects of social science and humanities, analytical ability.

Career possibilities: diplomatic worker, international businessperson.

Law

Describes the principles and procedures of legislation, decisions, regulations, and orders developed and enforced by institutions of government.

Levels offered: Doctoral.

Typical courses: Torts, Legal Research, Civil Procedure, Contracts, Criminal Law.

Related/complementary majors: Business, English, Political Science and Government, Speech, Conflict Resolution.

Needed abilities: excellent oral and written communication skills, strong analytical ability, good problem-solving skills, orientation to details.

Career possibilities: attorney.

Law Enforcement

Describes the theories, principles, and techniques of developing, administrating, and managing services for the safety and protection of people and property.

Levels offered: Associate, Bachelor's.

Typical courses: Police and Society, Criminal Law, Juvenile Justice System, Police Emergency Response Procedures, Police Intelligence.

Related/complementary majors: Criminal Justice.

Needed abilities: aptitude for applied science and law, analytical ability, problem-solving skills.

Career possibilities: police officer, corrections/parole/probation officer.

Legal Assisting/Paralegal

Prepares individuals to assist professional lawyers or to work in court houses.

Levels offered: Associate.

Typical courses: Legal Research and Writing, Probate Law, Litigation Procedures, Legal Environment of Business.

Related/complementary majors: Office Technology.

Needed abilities: good interpersonal and communication skills, orientation for details, analytical ability, ability to work independently as well as under the direction of an attorney.

Career possibilities: legal assistant or paralegal.

Legal Secretary

Prepares individuals to prepare legal papers and correspondence, such as summonses, complaints, motions, and subpoenas.

Levels offered: Associate.

Typical courses: Legal Document Processing, Records Management, Legal terminology and Concepts, Business Communications.

Related/complementary majors: Office Technology.

Needed abilities: secretarial skills or aptitude, orientation to details, ability to work accurately and precisely under the direction of an attorney.

Career possibilities: legal secretary.

Library and Information Science

Prepares professionals to process library materials and operate libraries.

Levels offered: Master's, with a limited number of Bachelor's and Doctoral programs.

Typical courses: Abstracting Services, Library Personnel Administration, Media Librarianship, Seminar on Indexing, Bibliography of Science, Engineering, and Technology.

Related/complementary majors: Information Science.

Needed abilities: good organizational skills, orientation for details, analytical ability, problem-solving skills.

Career possibilities: librarian, archivist, researcher.

Library Technology

Prepares individuals to assist professional librarians.

Levels offered: Associate.

Typical courses: Library Resources and Services, Children's Library Services, Cataloging, Information Retrieval for Library Technicians, Ordering and Receiving Library Materials.

Related/complementary majors: Office Technology.

Needed abilities: computer and clerical aptitude.

Career possibilities: library technician.

Linguistics

Describes the descriptive, historical, and theoretical aspects of language, its nature, structure, varieties. and development, including sound systems (phonology), grammatical systems (morphology, syntax), lexical systems (vocabulary, semology), and writing systems.

Levels offered: Bachelor's, Master's, Doctoral.

Typical courses: Historical and Comparative Linguistics, Developmental Linguistics, Structure of English, Semantics, Syntax and Lexical Analysis.

Related/complementary majors: English, Foreign Languages.

Needed abilities: excellent ear for and understanding of language, analytical ability.

Career possibilities: teacher, translator, writer/researcher.

Literature (American and British)

Describes writings in English (British or American) in prose or verse, especially those of an imaginative or critical character, including biography, drama, essay, criticism, fiction, poetry, myths, and legends.

Levels offered: Bachelor's, Master's, Doctoral.

Typical courses: Literature of the American West, Science Fiction and Fantasy, 20th Century American Novel, Modern British Writers, 16th Century English Poetry and Prose.

Related/complementary majors: English, Comparative Literature.

Needed abilities: excellent English language skills, analytical ability.

Career possibilities: teacher, writer.

Logistics/Operations/Supply Chain Management

Describes the design, control, and operations of supply chains in domestic and global markets, focusing on the procurement, production, and delivery of products and services to customers.

Levels offered: Bachelor's, Master's, Doctoral (limited number).

Typical courses: Quality Management and Measuring, Outsource Decisions, Forecasting in the Supply Chain, Information Technology Tools, Research and Negotiation.

Related/complementary majors: Business Administration and Management, Business Economics, Operations Management, Marketing.

Needed abilities: aptitude for all aspects of business, analytical ability, problem-solving skills.

Career possibilities: logistics planner, buyer, inventory specialist, supply management analyst.

Management Information Systems

Describes computer-based information systems that deal with business data and are generally characterized by logical patterns of clerical work flow from the point of original data gathering to completion of necessary reports and retrieval displays.

Levels offered: Bachelor's, Master's, Doctoral.

Typical courses: Systems Analysis, Introduction to Systems Concepts, Cases in MIS, Contemporary Topics in MIS.

Related/complementary majors: Business Administration and Management, Information Sciences and Management Systems.

Needed abilities: excellent aptitude for mathematics and logical thinking, analytical ability, problem-solving skills.

Career possibilities: business manager, information manager, systems analyst.

Management Science

Describes the application of mathematical and analytical techniques such as modeling, programming, forecasting, and analysis in the design, implementation, monitoring and control of organizational processes and operations to determine their purpose and effectiveness, and means for attaining maximum efficiency.

Levels offered: Bachelor's, Master's, Doctoral.

Typical courses: Operations Research for Decision Making, Linear Programming, Network Analysis and Dynamic Programming, Management Planning and Control, Systems Simulation.

Related/complementary majors: Computer Science, Operations Research.

Needed abilities: excellent aptitude for business and mathematics, analytical ability, problem-solving skills.

Career possibilities: business planner, business statistician, researcher.

Manufacturing Technology

Prepares individuals to technically assist in the design, construction, and application of machinery, tools, equipment, and processes used in the production of goods.

Levels offered: Associate, Bachelor's.

Typical courses: Production Control, Work Simplification and Measurement, Robots in Manufacturing, Quality Systems, Plastics Processing Technology.

Related/complementary majors: Industrial Technology, Quality Control Technology.

Needed abilities: good aptitude for applied physics and mathematics, analytical ability, problem-solving skills.

Career possibilities: manufacturing technician, production manager.

Marine Biology

Describes the nature and interrelationships of salt-water organisms and their aquatic environments.

Levels offered: Bachelor's, Master's, Doctoral.

Typical courses: Marine Ecology, Advanced Biology of Marine

Invertebrates, Behavior of Marine Organisms, Caribbean Organisms, Functional Morphology.

Related/complementary majors: Oceanography, Biology, Ecology.

Needed abilities: excellent aptitude for biological science, aptitude for chemistry, analytical ability.

Career possibilities: researcher, aquarium director.

Marketing

Describes the anticipation and control of demand through conception, promotion, exchange, and distribution of goods and services.

Levels offered: Associate, Bachelor's, Master's, Doctoral.

Typical courses: Advertising Management, Survey Sampling, International Marketing, Consumer Behavior, Marketing Channels Management.

Related/complementary majors: Business Administration and Management, Economics, International Business, Psychology.

Needed abilities: aptitude for business principles and applied psychology, analytical ability, problem-solving skills, creativity.

Career possibilities: marketing manager, marketing researcher, account executive.

Marriage and Family Counseling

Prepares individuals to diagnose and treat factors affecting marital or parent-child relationships, such as economic problems, illness, death, or divorce.

Levels offered: Master's, Doctoral.

Typical courses: Marital and Family Transaction, Family Development, Counseling Aspects of Sexuality, Marital Counseling and Divorce, Early Adulthood and Middle Age.

Related/complementary majors: Psychology, Social Work.

Needed abilities: excellent interpersonal and communication skills, aptitude for psychosocial science, analytical ability, problem-solving skills.

Career possibilities: marriage and family counselor.

Materials Engineering

Describes the structures, reactions, functions, and synthesis of metals, ceramics, plastics, textiles, pulp and paper, wood, and other materials.

Levels offered: Bachelor's, Master's, Doctoral.

Typical courses: Structures and Properties of Solids, Thermodynamics of Material Systems, Corrosion: Fundamentals and Applications, Electrical Properties and Materials, Manufacturing Processing and Materials.

Related/complementary majors: Ceramic Engineering, Forestry Production and Processing, Metallurgical Engineering, Metallurgy, Physical Chemistry, Physics, Textile Engineering.

Needed abilities: excellent aptitude for chemistry, physics, and mathematics, analytical ability, problem-solving skills.

Career possibilities: engineer, manufacturing manager.

Mathematics Education

Describes the theories, methods, and techniques involved in teaching the subject matter of mathematics.

Levels offered: Bachelor's, Master's, Doctoral.

Typical courses: Mathematics in the Elementary School, Mathematics Curriculum Development, Mathematics Methods and Materials, Computing in Mathematics Education, Mathematics for Exceptional Students.

Related/complementary majors: Education (Elementary, Middle, Secondary, Adult, Exceptional), Mathematics.

Needed abilities: excellent interpersonal and communication skills, excellent aptitude for mathematics, analytical ability, problem-solving skills.

Career possibilities: mathematics teacher.

Mathematics, General

Describes the sciences of logical symbolic languages and their applications.

Levels offered: Associate, Bachelor's, Master's, Doctoral.

Typical courses: Linear Algebra, Discrete Math, Differential and Riemannian Geometry, Statistical Inference, Computer Modeling.

Complementary majors: Computer Science.

Needed abilities: excellent aptitude for all aspects of mathematics, analytical ability, logical thinking skills.

Career possibilities: mathematician, cryptologist, operations research analyst, statistician.

Mechanical Design Technology

Prepares individuals to assist a mechanical or equipment-systems engineer in designing, detailing, producing, and testing machines.

Levels offered: Associate, Master's.

Typical courses: Internal Combustion Engines, Fluid Power Transmission, Design and Engineering Graphics, Mechanical Design, Engineering Design.

Related/complementary majors: Drafting and Design Technology.

Needed abilities: aptitude for applied physics and mathematics, good visual-spatial perception, analytical ability, problem-solving skills and creativity, orientation to details, ability to work under precise standards under the direction of an engineer.

Career possibilities: mechanical design technician, mechanical engineering assistant.

Mechanical Engineering

Describes the design, construction, maintenance, and operation of mechanical products and related systems, including production machinery, energy conversion devices, and vehicles.

Levels offered: Bachelor's, Master's, Doctoral.

Typical courses: Mechanics of Stability, Engineering Materials Science, Acoustics and Noise Control, Energy Conversion, Propulsion Systems.

Related/complementary majors: Engineering Mechanics, Industrial Engineering.

Needed abilities: excellent aptitude for physics and mathematics, analytical ability, problem-solving skills and creativity.

Career possibilities: automotive designer, mechanical engineer, production manager.

Medical Assisting

Prepares individuals to assist a physician by performing functions related to both business administration and clinical duties of a medical office.

Levels offered: Associate.

Typical courses: Pharmacology in Medical Assisting, Medical Terminology, Medical Assisting Techniques, Medical Records.

Related/complementary majors: Medical Office Technology.

Needed abilities: moderate aptitude for applied medical science and terminology, excellent interpersonal skills, organizational skills, orientation to details, ability to work precisely, ability to work under the direction of a physician.

Career possibilities: medical assistant, medical office manager.

Medical Illustration

Prepares individuals to demonstrate medical facts by the creation of illustrations, models, and teaching films.

Levels offered: Master's.

Typical courses: Electronic Media and Medical Illustration, Medical Photography, Surgical Observation and Sketching, Publication Art, Tri-Dimensional Techniques.

Related/complementary majors: Anatomy, Drawing, Film, Illustration Design, Photography, Video.

Needed abilities: aptitude for biological science, eye for visual detail, drawing ability.

Career possibilities: medical illustrator.

Medical Laboratory Technology

Prepares individuals to assist with biological and chemical tests.

Levels offered: Associate.

Typical courses: Phlebotomy, Blood Bank Theories and Techniques, Basic Concepts of Hematology, Clinical Serological Techniques and Applications.

Related/complementary majors: Biology, Chemistry.

Needed abilities: aptitude for applied biological and chemical sciences, analytical ability, orientation for visual details, ability to wonder precisely.

Career possibilities: medical lab technician.

Medical Office Management Technology

Prepares individuals to perform office duties in a medical setting.

Levels offered: Associate.

Typical courses: Medical Terminology, Computers in Medical Practice, Principles of Medical Coding and Billing, Medical Transcription.

Related/complementary majors: Office Technology.

Needed abilities: office skills, ability to work accurately, orientation to details.

Career possibilities: medical office manager, records technician, coder, medical biller, scheduler, receptionist.

Medical Technology

Prepares individuals as highly skilled laboratory scientists with a strong generalist orientation and an ability to perform complex and specialized procedures in all majors areas of the clinical laboratory.

Levels offered: Bachelor's, Master's.

Typical courses: Hematology, Immunology and Serology, Laboratory Management, General Clinical Chemistry, Molecular Diagnostics.

Related/complementary majors: Bacteriology, Biology, Chemistry, Microbiology, Pathology.

Needed abilities: excellent aptitude for the biological and chemical sciences, strong analytical ability, orientation for visual details, ability to work according to precise standards.

Career possibilities: medical technologist, lab director.

Medical Transcription

Prepares individuals to transcribe the oral reports of physicians into permanent written records.

Levels offered: Associate.

Typical courses: Medical Terminology, Proofreading, Advanced Word Processing, Co-op (Medical Transcription).

Related/complementary majors: Medical Office Management Technology.

Needed abilities: good listening skills, strong word processing skills, fast keyboarding speed, good spelling and grammar.

Career possibilities: medical transcriptionist.

Medicine

Describes the principles and procedures used in the observation, diagnosis, care, and treatment of illness, disease, injury, or deformity in humans.

Levels offered: Doctoral.

Typical courses: Gross Anatomy, General Pathology, Family Medicine, Organ System Pathology, Preventive Medicine and Community Health.

Related/complementary courses: Anatomy, Pathology, Pharmacology, Physiology, Psychology.

Needed abilities: excellent aptitude for biological, chemical, physical, and psychological sciences, excellent interpersonal skills, analytical ability, problem-solving skills, good manual dexterity.

Career possibilities: medical doctor.

Medieval and Renaissance Studies

Describes European civilization during the period from the fall of Rome through the Renaissance.

Levels offered: Bachelor's, Master's, Doctoral.

Typical courses: early Medieval Culture, Renaissance Literature, Chaucer, Culture of the High Middle Ages, Renaissance Arts.

Related/complementary majors: Art History and Appreciation, Comparative Literature, History, Music History and Appreciation, Philosophy, Religion, Museum Studies.

Needed abilities: excellent aptitude for social studies, arts, and letters,, analytical ability.

Career possibilities: museum curator, teacher.

Metal/Jewelry

Prepares individuals to design and fabricate art and jewelry from gems and precious metals.

Levels offered: Bachelor's, Master's.

Typical courses: Engraving, Stone Setting, History of Jewelry and Design, Metal Forming, Enameling.

Related/complementary majors: Fine Arts.

Needed abilities: high degree of creativity, excellent manual dexterity, eye for artistic detail.

Career possibilities: jewelry designer, jeweler.

Metallurgical Engineering

Describes the development and control of processes for extraction of metals from their ores and metal refining, the properties of metals and alloys, and the manufacturing and processing of metals.

Levels offered: Bachelor's, Master's, Doctoral.

Typical courses: Phase Transformations in Solids, Fundamentals of Electrochemistry, Solidification Processing of Fusion Welding, Transport Properties, Physical Chemistry of Metallurgical Reactions.

Related/complementary courses: Metallurgy, Physical Chemistry, Physics.

Needed abilities: excellent aptitude for physical science and mathematics, analytical ability, problem-solving skills.

Career possibilities: metallurgical engineer.

Microbiology

Describes microorganisms including bacteria, viruses, protozoa, and certain fungi.

Levels offered: Bachelor's, Master's, Doctoral.

Typical courses: Genetics of Bacteria, Microbial Diversity, Applied Microbial Biotechnology, Virology, Comparative Anatomy and Physiology of Bacteria.

Related/complementary majors: Bacteriology, Biology, Medical Technology.

Needed abilities: excellent aptitude for biological science, analytical ability.

Career possibilities: scientist, lab worker.

Middle Eastern Studies

Describes the history, society, politics, culture, and economics of countries lying east of the Mediterranean and Aegean Seas to India.

Levels offered: Bachelor's, Master's, Doctoral.

Typical courses: Modern Iran, Arabic Folklore, Persian Epic, Biblical Hebrew, Educational Issues and the Third World.

Related/complementary majors: Anthropology, Art History and Appreciation, Comparative Literature, History, International Studies. Music History and Appreciation, Political Science, Religion, Sociology.

Needed abilities: aptitude for social science, history, religion, political science, analytical ability.

Career possibilities: diplomat, international businessperson.

Middle School Education

Describes the theories, methods, and techniques of designing, implementing, and evaluating, organized learning activities for students at the middle school level.

Levels offered: Bachelor's, Master's, Doctoral.

Typical courses: Psychology of Early Adolescence, Career Education and Guidance in Middle School, Curriculum Development in Middle School, Philosophy and Organization of Middle School.

Related/complementary majors: Specific subject areas.

Needed abilities: excellent interpersonal and communication skills, analytical ability, problem-solving skills.

Career possibilities: middle school teacher.

Military Science

Describes the purpose and objectives of the United States Military and its branches, customs, rank structure, and traditions, and its importance in national defense and security.

Levels offered: Bachelor's.

Typical courses: American Defense Policy, Introduction to Leadership Dynamics, Advanced Military Science, Military Administration and Logistic Management.

Related/complementary majors: Management Science, History, Geography, Physical Science, Political Science.

Needed abilities: ability to understand and apply information relating to all aspects of the military, strong leadership ability, physical capabilities.

Career possibilities: military officer, civilian worker for the Department of Defense.

Missionary Studies

Provides students with the knowledge and skills to carry Christian gospel to persons of every race, nation, and religion.

Levels offered: Bachelor's, Master's.

Typical courses: Perspectives on World Evangelism, Church Planting, History of Missions, Teaching Bible, Missions Practicum.

Related/complementary majors: Anthropology, Area and Ethnic Studies, Bible Studies, Foreign Language, Religion, Religious Education.

Needed abilities: understanding of and commitment to organized religion, good interpersonal skills, interest in other cultures and religions.

Career possibilities: missionary, religious worker.

Mortuary Science

Trains individuals to perform preparations for embalming or cremation for interment in conformity with legal requirements, and to run a funeral home or related business.

Levels offered: Associate.

Typical courses: Embalming Theory and Practice, Funeral Service Counseling, Restorative Art, Anatomy and Physiology, Mortuary Administration and Funeral Management.

Related/complementary courses: Business Management.

Needed abilities: moderate aptitude for applied biology and chemistry, analytical ability, problem-solving skills, moderate manual dexterity, good interpersonal skills, aptitude for business.

Career possibilities: embalmer, funeral home director.

Museum Studies

Prepares students to develop, organize, administer, store, retrieve, and facilitate the use of museums and museums materials.

Levels offered: Master's, Doctoral (limited number of programs).

Typical courses: Museum Administration and Ethics, Curatorial

Practices, Museum Education, Collections Management, History and Futures of Museums.

Related/complementary majors: Archival Science, Anthropology, Area and Ethnic Studies, Archaeology, Astronomy, Biology, Crafts and Design, Fine Arts, History, Marine Biology/Oceanography, Visual Arts, Public Administration.

Needed abilities: understanding and appreciation of social science, natural science, or visual art, analytical ability, organizational skills. managerial abilities.

Career possibilities: museum curator/director.

Music Education

Describes the theories, methods, and techniques involved in teaching the subject matter of music.

Levels offered: Bachelor's, Master's, Doctoral.

Typical courses: Conducting and Arranging, Music in the Elementary Grades, Piano, Models of Music Teaching, Survey of Music History.

Related/complementary majors: Education; Music, General; Music History and Appreciation; Music performance.

Needed abilities: excellent interpersonal and communication skills, excellent aptitude for music, analytical ability, problem-solving skills.

Music, General

Includes music history and appreciation, music performance, music theory and composition.

Levels offered: Associate, Bachelor's.

Typical courses: Survey of Music Literature, Concert Attendance, Music Performance, Piano, Ear Training.

Related/complementary majors: Music History, Music Performance, Music Theory and Composition.

Needed abilities: aptitude for all aspects of music.

Career possibilities: music teacher, performer.

Music History and Literature

Describes music and its relationship to concurrent events, the evolution of musical styles, the lives of musicians, and the role of music in human affairs, including contemporary times.

Levels offered: Bachelor's, Master's, Doctoral.

Typical courses: History of Opera, Music of the Baroque, Music of the Classic Period, Music of Asia.

Related/complementary majors: Area and Ethnic Studies, History, Psychology, Sociology.

Needed abilities: ability to apply psychological, sociological, and historical analysis to music, ear for various aspects of music, analytical ability.

Career possibilities: music critic, music historian, music librarian.

Music Management

Prepares individuals to apply economic and business principles to the management and operation of profit and nonprofit music organizations, groups, or individuals.

Levels offered:

Typical courses: Talent Agencies and Management, Art and Business of Recording, Music Publishing, Concert Promotion, Music and Sound Industry Marketing.

Related/complementary majors: Business Administration, Marketing.

Needed abilities: understanding of music, aptitude for business, analytical ability, problem-solving skills, good interpersonal skills.

Career possibilities: agent, business manager, promoter.

Music Performance

Describes the applied study of and performance on musical instruments or voice and vocal performance, either solo or in ensemble.

Levels offered: Associate, Bachelor's, Master's, Doctoral.

Typical courses: Lyric Diction, Small Ensembles, Piano, Percussion, Strings.

Related/complementary majors: Music History, Music Theory and Composition.

Needed abilities: musical ability (instrumental or vocal), creativity.

Career possibilities: musician, teacher.

Music Theory and Composition

Describes the principles, forms, and foundations of music as well as the techniques of creating and arranging tonal combinations and sequences.

Levels offered: Bachelor's, Master's, Doctoral.

Typical courses: Analysis of Tonal Music, Creative Composition, 18th Century Counterpoint Theory, Analysis of 20th Century Music.

Related/complementary courses: Music History and Literature.

Needed abilities: excellent aptitude for musical foundations, analytical ability, creativity.

Career possibilities: composer, musical arranger.

Music Therapy

Prepares individuals to use individual and group musical activities with physically and mentally ill individuals to accomplish therapeutic goals.

Levels offered: Bachelor's, Master's, Doctoral.

Typical courses: Psychological Foundations of Music, Influence of Music on Behavior, Music for Group Activities, Introduction to Music in Therapy, Music Therapy Practicum.

Related/complementary majors: Art Therapy, Dance/Movement Therapy, Recreational Therapy.

Needed abilities: excellent interpersonal skills, musical aptitude (voice/instrument), analytical ability, problem-solving skills, creativity.

Career possibilities: music therapist.

Musicology

Focuses on the systematic study on the forms and methods of music and the functions of music in Western and non–Western cultures.

Levels offered: Bachelor's (limited number of programs), Master's, Doctoral.

Typical courses: Bibliography and Methodology, Scholarly Writing and Research Techniques, World Music Ensemble, Critical Theory, Historiography, Analysis, and Interpretation.

Related courses: Music History and Literature, Music Theory and Composition, Area and Ethnic Studies.

Needed abilities: excellent understanding of all aspects of music, analytical ability.

Career possibilities: researcher, teacher, music librarian.

Naval Architecture and Marine Engineering

Describes the principles and techniques of design, construction, installation, maintenance, and operation of vehicles and equipment operating on or in the water.

Levels offered: Bachelor's, Master's, Doctoral.

Typical courses: Marine Structures, Hydromechanics, Marine Construction Materials, Ship Structure and Stability, Analysis and Design of Structures.

Related/complementary majors: Ocean Engineering, Mechanical Engineering.

Needed abilities: excellent aptitude for physics and mathematics, analytical ability, problem-solving skills.

Career possibilities: boat designer, marine engineer.

Naval Science

Describes the purpose and objectives of the United States Navy and Marine Corps and all its branches, its rank structure, its traditions and customs, and its importance in national security.

Levels offered: Bachelor's.

Typical courses: Seapower and Maritime Affairs, Navigation and Naval Operations, Amphibious Warfare, Leadership, and Management. Naval Ship Systems.

Related/complementary courses: Physical Science, Geography, Management Science, Military Science.

Needed abilities: strong leadership ability, ability to understand and apply information relating to all aspects of the Marines or Navy.

Career possibilities: Naval or Marine officer, civilian worker for the Department of Defense.

Neurosciences

Describes the anatomy, physiology, biochemistry, and molecular biology of nerves and nervous tissues and their relation to behavior and learning.

Levels offered: Master's, Doctoral.

Typical courses: Developmental Neurobiology, Behavioral Neurophysiology, Instrumentation Methods in Neurophysiology, Regeneration in the Nervous System, Biological Basis of Neuropharmacology.

Related/complementary majors: Anatomy, Biochemistry, Physiological Psychology, Physiology.

Needed abilities: excellent aptitude for biochemistry, anatomy, physiology, and psychology, analytical ability.

Career possibilities: neuroscience researcher or lab technician.

Nuclear Engineering

Describes the design, development, manufacture, construction, installation, maintenance, and repair of mechanical plants and equipment for the release, control, and utilization of nuclear energy.

Levels offered: Bachelor's, Master's, Doctoral.

Typical courses: Nuclear Fuel Cycles, Thermal Aspects of Nuclear Reactors, Nuclear Materials, Fusion Reactor Engineering, Dynamics of Nuclear Systems.

Related/complementary majors: Nuclear Physics.

Needed abilities: excellent aptitude for physics and mathematics, analytical ability, problem-solving skills.

Career possibilities: nuclear engineer.

Nuclear Medical Technology

Describes the preparation and administration of radioactive isotopes, and the measurement of glandular and other bodily activity in therapeutic and diagnostic studies.

Levels offered: Associate, Bachelor's.

Typical courses: Radiation Biology, Radionuclide Therapy, Instrumentation and Computers in Nuclear Medicine, Radiation Health safety, Radioassay.

Related/complementary majors: Radiation Technology, Biochemistry, Biophysics, Physiology.

Needed abilities: aptitude for biology, chemistry, and physics, ability to operate computers and complex machinery, good interpersonal skills.

Career possibilities: nuclear medicine technologist.

Nuclear Physics

Describes the intrinsic properties of nucleons and the nucleon-nuclear interactions, nuclear models, and nuclear reactions.

Levels offered: Master's, Doctoral.

Typical courses: Quantum Theory and Nuclear Force, Nuclear Decay Processes, Nuclear Reactions, Nuclear Properties.

Related/complementary majors: Nuclear Engineering.

Needed abilities: excellent aptitude for physical science and mathematics, analytical ability.

Career possibilities: physicist.

Nuclear Technologies

Prepares individuals to support professionals engaged in developing, manufacturing, testing, researching, maintaining, storing, and handling materials in the nuclear science and energy field.

Levels offered: Associate, Bachelor's (limited number of programs).

Typical courses: Radiation Detection and Measurement, Radiation Protection, Radiation Biophysics, Neutron Activation Analysis, Nuclear Instrumentation.

Related/complementary majors: Biophysics, Physics.

Needed abilities: aptitude for physics, analytical ability, problem-solving skills, orientation to details, ability to work under the direction of a nuclear engineer or other professional.

Career possibilities: nuclear engineering assistant, nuclear technician.

Nursing

Describes the techniques and procedures for providing care for sick, disabled, or other individuals, including the administering of medications and treatments, assisting physicians during examinations and treatment, and planning education for health maintenance.

Levels offered: Associate, Bachelor's, Master's, Doctoral.

Typical courses: Community Health Nursing, Psychopathology, Principles of Pharmacology, Clinical Nutrition, Medical-Surgical Nursing.

Related/complementary majors: Gerontology, Health Care Administration, Health Education, Physiology, Public Health.

Needed abilities: aptitude for biology and chemistry, analytical ability, problem-solving skills, excellent interpersonal skills, orientation to details, ability to work precisely, ability to work both independently and under the direction of a physician.

Career possibilities: nurse, health educator, health care manager.

Nutrition/Dietetics

Prepares students to assist others in maximizing health by making better nutritional choices.

Levels offered: Bachelor's, Master's, Doctoral.

Typical courses: Nutrition in the Lifecycle, Quantity Food Procurement and Preparation, Nutritional Aspects of Biochemistry, Nutrition Counseling, Medical Nutrition Therapy.

Related/complementary majors: Biochemistry, Public Health.

Needed abilities: aptitude for biological and chemical science, good interpersonal skills, analytical ability, problem-solving skills.

Career possibilities: health care dietician, food service manager.

Occupational Health and Safety Technology

Prepares individuals to work with safety engineers and managers in analyzing working conditions in places of employment to ensure maximum safety to workers and occupations.

Levels offered: Associate, Bachelor's, Master's.

Typical courses: Industrial Environmental Monitoring, Industrial Fire Protection, Administration and Supervision of Safety Programs, Industrial ventilation for Environmental Health and Safety, Industrial Audiology.

Related/complementary majors: Environmental Health Engineering, Industrial Engineering.

Needed abilities: aptitude for applied biological and physical science, analytical ability, problem-solving skills.

Career possibilities: occupational health and safety manager or technician.

Occupational Therapy

Prepares individuals to use the principles and techniques of providing purposeful activities and exercise to evaluate and treat mental, physical, or emotional dysfunction and illness in children and adults.

Levels offered: Master's, Doctoral.

Typical courses: Occupational Therapy for Children with Developmental Delays, Occupational Therapy Theory in Aging, Activities for Therapeutic Intervention, Therapeutic Techniques in Psychosocial Practice, Human Adaptation in Physical Disabilities and Chronic Disease.

Related/complementary majors: Art Therapy, Dance Therapy, Exercise Physiology, Music Therapy, Orthotics/Prosthetics, Physical Therapy, Physiology, Psychology, Recreational Therapy, Speech-Language Pathology.

Needed abilities: aptitude for psychological and biological sciences, analytical ability, problem-solving skills, creativity, excellent interpersonal skills, good manual dexterity and physical stamina.

Career possibilities: occupational therapist.

Occupational Therapy Assisting

Prepares individuals to assist occupational therapists in providing purposeful activities and exercise to evaluate and treat mental, physical, or emotional dysfunction and illness in children and adults.

Levels offered: Associate.

Typical courses: Human Growth and Development, Therapeutic Use of Crafts, Medical Terminology, Pediatric Occupational Therapy, Occupational Therapy with the Aging.

Related/complementary courses: Physical Therapy Assisting.

Needed abilities: aptitude for psychological and biological sciences, problem-solving skills, creativity, excellent interpersonal skills, physical stamina.

Career possibilities: occupational therapy assistant.

111

Ocean Engineering

Describes wave action upon sea structures, equipment, and materials, including the developing of instrumentation to determine the forces and acceleration of such actions.

Levels offered: Bachelor's, Master's, Doctoral.

Typical courses: Dynamics of the Ocean, Ocean Acoustics, Ocean Wave Mechanics, Ocean Measurements.

Related/complementary majors: Naval Architecture and Marine Engineering, Oceanography, Physics.

Needed abilities: excellent aptitude for physical science and mathematics, analytical ability, strong problem-solving skills.

Career possibilities: ocean engineer/researcher.

Oceanographic Technology

Prepares individuals to understand the specialized equipment, instruments, and techniques determining the depth, temperature, chemical composition, and rate and direction of flow of underwater currents in ocean, seas, or other major bodies of water.

Levels offered: Associate, Bachelor's (limited number of programs).

Typical courses: Aquaculture, Ocean Sampling, Introduction to Ocean Engineering, Navigation and Seamanship.

Related/complementary majors: Instrumentation Technology.

Needed abilities: aptitude for applied physics, analytical ability, problem-solving skills, orientation to details, ability to work precisely and under the direction of an oceanographer or ocean engineer.

Career possibilities: oceanography technician, research assistant.

Oceanography

Describes the ocean and its phenomena, including the physical and chemical properties of water; the topography and composition of the ocean bottom; waves, currents, and tides; and the formation of the ocean.

Levels offered: Bachelor's, Master's, Doctoral.

Typical courses: Marine Sedimentation, Oceanographic Instrumentation, Barrier Islands and Beaches, Marine Ecosystems.

Related/complementary majors: Marine Biology, Ocean Engineering.

Needed abilities: excellent aptitude for chemistry and physical science, analytical ability.

Career possibilities: oceanographer,

Office Supervision and Management

Prepares individuals to supervise employees; budget, analyze, and coordinate clerical and other office activities; evaluate, organize, and/or revise office operations and procedures to establish uniformity in handling correspondence, records, and other materials; and design various office layouts to facilitate maximum productivity and efficiency.

Levels offered: Associate.

Typical courses: Business Policies, Records and Database Management, Human Relations, Principles of Management, Accounting.

Related/complementary majors: Business Administration and Management, Information Sciences and Systems, Secretarial and Related Programs.

Needed abilities: aptitude for business, ability to supervise others, analytical ability, problem-solving skills, understanding of office procedures.

Career possibilities: office manager, business manager, administration assistant.

Operations Research

Describes the principles and procedures of analyzing management problems, using probability theory, continuous distributions, mathematical programming, queuing theory, Markov processors, replacement maintenance and inventory models, and simulation and game theory.

Levels offered: Master's, Doctoral.

Typical courses: Research Methodology, Computer Techniques for Quantitative Analysis, Probabilistic Models, Linear Programming, Statistical Decision Making.

Related/complementary majors: Business Administration and

Management, Business Statistics, Information Science, Management Science.

Needed abilities: excellent aptitude for business, mathematics, and logical thinking, analytical ability.

Career possibilities: business analyst, management consultant.

Optics

Describes the nature and propagation of light.

Levels offered: Master's, Doctoral.

Typical courses: Quantum Optics, Geometric Optics, wave Optics, Optics of Transformation.

Related/complementary majors: Engineering Physics.

Needed abilities: excellent aptitude for physical science and mathematics, analytical ability.

Career possibilities: optical engineer/physicist.

Optometric Technology

Prepares individuals to perform a variety of vision care procedures under the supervision of an optometrist.

Levels offered: Associate.

Typical courses: Optometric Office Procedures, Contact Lenses, Developmental Vision/Vision Therapy, Ophthalmic Optics, Ocular Anatomy and Physiology.

Related/complementary majors: Medical Assisting.

Needed abilities: aptitude for applied anatomy, physiology, and physics, good interpersonal skills, orientation to details, ability to work with precision under the direction of an optometrist.

Career possibilities: optometric technician.

Optometry

Describes the principles and techniques for testing, determining defects, and prescribing corrective means for deficiencies in an individual's vision.

Levels offered: Doctoral.

Typical courses: Ocular Disease, Vision Therapy, Contact Lenses, Physiological Optics: Binocular Function, Ocular Microbiology.

Related/complementary majors: Anatomy, neurosciences, Physics, Physiology.

Needed abilities: excellent aptitude for biology and physics, strong analytical ability, strong problem-solving skills, good interpersonal skills, orientation to details, ability to work precisely.

Career possibilities: optometrist.

Organic Chemistry

Describes the hydrocarbons and the derivatives, either synthetic or produced by living organisms, including the isolation, compositions, structures, physical and spectroscopic properties, syntheses, energy relationships, and chemical transformations of these substances.

Levels offered: Master's, Doctoral.

Typical courses: Physical Organic Chemistry, Advanced Organic Syntheses, Spectroscopic Identification and Qualitative Organic Analysis, Structure and Reactions in Organic Chemistry.

Related/complementary majors: Pharmaceutical Chemistry.

Needed abilities: excellent aptitude for chemical science, analytical ability.

Career possibilities: chemist.

Organizational Behavior

Describes the behavior and motivations of individuals functioning in groups, the influence of styles of leadership that may be used by managers, and the means of intervention that may be used to improve interpersonal relations and team behavior.

Levels offered: Master's, Doctoral.

Typical courses: Productivity and Strategy, Industrial and Labor Relations, Operations Management, Legal and Social Frameworks for Managerial Policy, Statistics for Business Control.

Related/complementary majors: Business Administration and Management, Human Resources, Industrial and Organizational Psychology, Social Psychology, Sociology.

Needed abilities: strong aptitude for business management and social science, analytical ability, problem-solving skills.

Career possibilities: business manager/consultant.

Orthotic/Prosthetic Assisting

Prepares individuals to assist the orthotist/prosthetist in caring for patients by making casts, measurements, and model specifications, and fitting supportive appliances and/or artificial limbs.

Levels offered: Associate.

Typical courses: Introduction to Prosthetic Materials, Lower Extremity Orthotics, Upper Extremity Prosthetics, Foot and Ankle Skeletal Structure.

Related/complementary courses: Occupational Therapy Assisting, Physical Therapy Assisting.

Needed abilities: aptitude for basic anatomy and physiology, ability to use tools and machines, good manual dexterity, ability to work with precision and deal with details, good interpersonal skills, analytical ability, some problem-solving skills.

Career possibilities: orthotic/prosthetic technician.

Orthotics/Prosthetics

Prepares individuals to care for patients by making casts, measurements, and molded specifications, and fitting supportive appliances and/or artificial limbs.

Levels offered: Bachelor's, Master's.

Typical courses: Prosthetic Tools and Materials, Related Anatomy of the Above-Knee Amputation, Spinal Orthotics, Orthotic Shoe Fabrication.

Related/complementary majors: Anatomy, Occupational Therapy, Physical Therapy, Bioengineering and Biomedical Engineering.

Needed abilities: aptitude for basic anatomy and physiology, analytical ability, problem-solving skills, ability to use tools and machines, good manual dexterity, ability to work with precision and deal with details, good interpersonal skills.

Career possibilities: orthotist, prosthetist.

Osteopathic Medicine

Describes the diagnosis and treatment of health problems through physical, medical, and surgical methods, with an emphasis on manipulation methods of detecting and correcting faulty body structure.

Levels offered: Doctoral.

Typical courses: Osteopathic Manipulative Medicine, Dermatology and Allergy, Rheumatology and Orthopedics, Behavioral Science and Medicine, Radiology

Related/complementary majors: Anatomy, Neurosciences, Pharmacology, Physiology.

Needed abilities: excellent aptitude for biological, physical, and psychological sciences, excellent interpersonal skills, analytical ability, problem-solving skills, good manual dexterity and physical strength.

Career possibilities: osteopathic physician.

Painting

Describes the aesthetic qualities, techniques, and processes for expressing emotions and communicating ideas through the application of paints to canvases or other materials.

Levels offered: Bachelor's, Master's.

Typical courses: Figure Painting, Watercolor, Painting Survey: Materials and Methods, Composition and Design for Painting.

Related/complementary majors: Art Education, Art History and Appreciation, Art Therapy, Drawing.

Needed abilities: artistic ability, creativity.

Career possibilities: art teacher or instructor, painter, commercial artist or illustrator.

Paleontology

Describes the fossil evidence of prehistoric life.

Levels offered: Master's, Doctoral.

Typical courses: Age of Dinosaurs, Fossils and the Record of Life, Floras in Space and Time, Ancient Climates, Evolution of Fishes.

Related/complementary majors: Geology, Biology, Earth Science.

Needed abilities: strong aptitude for natural science, analytical and research ability.

Career possibilities: museum curator, researcher.

Parks and Recreation Management

Prepares individuals to plan and maintain recreational facilities and programs for public or private agencies.

Levels offered: Associate, Bachelor's, Master's, Doctoral.

Typical courses: Public Land Use Practices, Camp Management, Legal and Financial Aspects of Recreational Service, Park System and Planning, Recreational Leadership.

Related/complementary majors: Business Administration, Public Administration.

Needed abilities: aptitude for social science and applied business practices, problem-solving skills, managerial ability.

Career possibilities: parks/recreation department manager, leisure planner, state recreational consultant.

Pathology, Human and Animal

Describes the nature, causes, and development of human and animal diseases.

Levels offered: Master's, Doctoral.

Typical courses: Immunology, Pathobiology, Molecular Biology of Connective Tissue, Hemostasis and Thrombosis.

Related/complementary majors: Anatomy, Biochemistry, Endocrinology, Microbiology, Neurosciences.

Needed abilities: excellent aptitude for biological science, analytical ability.

Career possibilities: clinical pathologist, researcher.

Peace Studies

Describes the peace development process, including the analysis of peace and war systems, dispute settlement techniques, social movements, world order studies, creative change facilitation, and conflict analysis and regulation.

Levels offered: Bachelor's, Master's.

Typical courses: Nuclear Safety, Theory of Nonviolence, Contemporary Processes in Central America, Technology, Doctrine, and Politics in the Nuclear Arms Race.

Related/complementary majors: Conflict/Dispute Analysis/

Management/Resolution, International Relations, Social Psychology, Political Science and Government.

Needed abilities: good aptitude for social science, analytical ability, problem-solving skills.

Career possibilities: mediator, diplomatic worker.

Personality Psychology

Describes the unique organization of the characteristics that set the individual apart from other individuals and, at the same time, determine how others respond to that person.

Levels offered: Master's, Doctoral.

Typical courses: Human Sexuality, Personality of Adolescents, Psychopathology, Psychology of Women.

Related/complementary majors: Clinical Psychology, Developmental Psychology, Psychometrics, Social Psychology.

Needed abilities: excellent aptitude for psychologist and social sciences, analytical ability.

Career possibilities: psychologist, psychology writer.

Petroleum Engineering

Describes the processes of recovering and refining crude oil and gas, including the design, development, construction, installation, maintenance, and repair of physical facilities.

Levels offered: Bachelor's, Master's, Doctoral.

Typical courses: Petroleum Reservoir Fluids, Evaluation of Oil and Gas Properties, Microcomputer Pipeline Engineering, Drilling and Design Production, Enhanced Oil Recovery.

Related/complementary majors: Geochemistry, Geological Engineering.

Needed abilities: excellent aptitude for physical science and mathematics, analytical ability, problem-solving skills.

Career possibilities: petroleum engineer.

Pharmaceutical Chemistry

Describes the chemical and physical properties of organic and inorganic compounds which have medicinal or pharmaceutical uses.

Levels offered: Master's, Doctoral.

Typical courses: Chemistry of Synthetic Drugs, Bioassay, Principles of Drug Design, Instrumental Methods of Drug Analysis, Physiological and Clinical Chemistry.

Related/complementary majors: Organic Chemistry, Inorganic Chemistry.

Needed abilities: excellent aptitude for chemistry, analytical ability.

Career possibilities: pharmaceutical chemist/researcher.

Pharmacology

Describes the therapeutic and toxic effects of drugs, including pharmodynamic behavior, metabolism, interactions with other chemicals, and the biochemical and physiological effects on humans and animals.

Levels offered: Master's, Doctoral.

Typical courses: Pharmacokinetics, Medical Biochemistry, Methods of Drug Action, Experimental Models, Laboratory Instrumentation.

Related/complementary majors: Biochemistry, Pathology, Pharmacy, Physiology.

Needed abilities: excellent aptitude for biology and chemistry, analytical ability.

Career possibilities: pharmacologist.

Pharmacy

Describes the principles and procedures of procuring, preparing, compounding, recommending, administering, and dispensing drugs, medicines, and devices used in the diagnosis, treatment, or prevention of diseases.

Levels offered: Doctoral.

Typical courses: Clinical Pharmacy and Therapeutics, Medicinal Chemistry, Pharmacy Law, Drug Literature Evaluation, Nonprescription Medications.

Related/complementary majors: Pharmacology, Pharmaceutical Chemistry.

Needed abilities: aptitude for biochemical science, analytical ability, problem-solving skills, orientation to details, ability to work precisely.

Career possibilities: pharmacist.

Philosophy

Describes the basic truths and principles of being and of knowledge.

Levels offered: Associate, Bachelor's, Master's, Doctoral.

Typical courses: Existentialism, Ethics, Ancient Philosophy, Philosophy of Art and Beauty, Chinese Philosophy.

Related/complementary majors: Religion.

Needed abilities: aptitude for synthesis of abstract information and theories, analytical ability, ability to express self well (both orally and in writing).

Career possibilities: teacher, writer.

Photographic Technology

Prepares individuals as highly skilled photographic technicians.

Levels offered: Associate, Bachelor's (limited number of programs).

Typical courses: Industrial Photography Instrumentation, Electrostatic Imaging Methods, Photographic Processes and Materials, Digital Photography Processing, Darkroom Techniques.

Related/complementary majors: Photography.

Needed abilities: aptitude for basic applied physics and chemistry, manual dexterity, eye for visual details, analytical ability, problem-solving skills.

Career possibilities: photographic technician.

Photography

Describes the historic development, aesthetic qualities, theories, techniques, and creative processes of producing images on photographic film or digitally.

Levels offered: Associate, Bachelor's, Master's.

Typical courses: Portrait Retouching, Photo Illustration, Photography of the Natural World, Color Photography, Commercial Photography.

Related/complementary majors: Film, Video, Illustration.

Needed abilities: eye for artistic detail, good problem-solving skills, high degree of creativity.

Career possibilities: photographer.

Physical Chemistry

Describes the theoretical and experimental investigation of matter, with emphasis on the most fundamental aspects of structure and bonding, and the relationships of the mechanics and energy changes of transformation.

Levels offered: Master's, Doctoral.

Typical courses: Chemical Kinetics, Thermodynamics, Bonding Theory, Organic Reactions and Synthesis.

Related/complementary majors: Chemistry, Physics, Chemical Engineering.

Needed abilities: excellent aptitude for chemical and physical sciences, analytical ability.

Career possibilities: chemist.

Physical Education

Describes the theories, methods, and techniques involved in teaching the subject matter of physical education.

Levels offered: Bachelor's, Master's, Doctoral.

Typical courses: Kinesiology, Physiology of Exercise, Volleyball, Gymnastics, Tests and Measurements in Physical Education.

Related/complementary majors: Education (Elementary of Secondary), Exercise Physiology/Science, Health Education, Sports Studies.

Needed abilities: excellent interpersonal and communication skills, aptitude for physiology, analytical ability, problem-solving skills, physical energy, stamina, and coordination.

Career possibilities: physical educator, coach, fitness instructor.

Physical Therapy

Prepares individuals to use the principles and techniques of treating disease, bodily weakness, or physical defects by physical remedies.

Levels offered: Master's, Doctoral.

Typical courses: Therapeutic Exercise, Pathophysiology, Research in Physical Therapy, Physical therapy Administration, Electrotherapy.

Related/complementary majors: Anatomy, Exercise Physiology, Physiology, Occupational Therapy, Sports Medicine.

Needed abilities: excellent aptitude for biological and physical science, analytical ability, problem-solving skills, creativity, excellent interpersonal skills, good physical stamina and strength.

Career possibilities: physical therapist.

Physical Therapy Assisting

Prepares individuals to assist a physical therapist in implementing the plan for physical therapy.

Levels offered: Associate.

Typical courses: Patient Management, Medical Terminology, Clinical Experience, Hydrotherapy, Therapeutic Exercise.

Related/complementary majors: biology, physics, occupational therapy.

Needed abilities: aptitude for biological and physical science, analytical ability, problem-solving, good interpersonal skills, good physical stamina and strength, ability to work under the direction of a physical therapist.

Career possibilities: physical therapy assistant.

Physician Assisting

Prepares individuals to perform physician-delegated functions in such areas as family medicine, internal medicine, obstetrics, emergency medicine.

Levels offered: Associate, Bachelor's, Master's.

Typical courses: Gross Anatomy, Medical Physiology, Emergency Care, Physical Diagnosis, Medical Interviewing.

Related/complementary majors: Anatomy, Physiology, Biomedical Science.

Needed abilities: excellent aptitude for biomedical science, problem-solving skills, excellent interpersonal skills, ability to work both independently and under the direction of a physician.

Career possibilities: physician assistant.

Physics, General

Describes the physical properties and interactions of matter and energy, including equilibrium, power, wave phenomena, mechanics, heat, electricity, magnetism, sound, lights, special relativity, and the particular nature of matter.

Levels offered: Associate, Bachelor's, Master's, Doctoral.

Typical courses: Electromagnetic Theory, Thermodynamics, Physics in Communications, Optics, Physics of Flight.

Related/complementary majors: Mathematics.

Needed abilities: excellent aptitude for physical science and mathematics, analytical ability.

Career possibilities: physicist (with a graduate degree), research assistant.

Physiological Psychology

Studies the processes that determine what actions will occur at a particular time, and the strength or precision with which those actions will occur.

Levels offered: Master's, Doctoral.

Typical courses: Hormonal Biochemistry, Neural and Behavioral Endocrinology, Biobehavioral Mechanisms of Stress and Disease, Psychopathology of Brain Function.

Related/complementary majors: Experimental Psychology, Neuroscience.

Needed abilities: strong aptitude for biological and psychological science, analytical ability.

Career possibilities: psychological researcher, biofeedback clinician.

Physiology

Describes living organisms or their parts, and their relationship to the restoration and preservation of good health.

Levels offered: Bachelor's, Master's, Doctoral.

Typical courses: Physiology of the Cell, Comparative Invertebrate Physiology, Renal and Hepatic Physiology, Animal Physiology, Neurobiology.

Related/complementary majors: Anatomy, Biology, Endocrinology, Exercise Physiology, Medicine, Neuroscience, Nursing, Zoology.

Needed abilities: excellent aptitude for biological science, analytical ability.

Career possibilities: scientist, researcher.

Planetary Sciences

Describes the geology of planets other than the earth.

Levels offered: Bachelor's, Master's, Doctoral.

Typical courses: Cosmochemistry, Evolution of Planetary Structures, Meteorites, Planetary Atmospheres, Planetary Geography.

Related/complementary majors: Astronomy, Earth Science, Geology, Geophysics.

Needed abilities: aptitude for natural science, analytical ability.

Career possibilities: astronaut, planetarium director, space scientist/researcher.

Plant Pathology

Describes the nature, causes, and development of plant diseases.

Levels offered: Bachelor's, Master's, Doctoral.

Typical courses: Microenvironment and Crop Growth, Fungi, Plant Stress, Viruses and Prokaryotes.

Related/complementary majors: Agronomy, Botany, Plant Protection.

Needed abilities: aptitude for biological and chemical science, analytical ability, problem-solving skills.

Career possibilities: plant consultant, plant researcher/scientist.

Plant Physiology

Describes the study of plant functions, including such metabolic processes as photosynthesis, respiration, assimilation, and transpiration.

Levels offered: Bachelor's, Master's, Doctoral.

Typical courses: Advanced Plant Breeding, Plant Growth and Development, Plant Metabolism, Soil-Plant Relationships.

Related/complementary majors: Agronomy, Biochemistry, Botany, Soil Sciences.

Needed abilities: aptitude for biological science, analytical ability.

Career possibilities: plant scientist, plant products sales representative.

Plant Protection

Describes the principles and practices of combining entomology, plant pathology, and weed science with crop production to minimize the economic loss caused by plant pests and to protect the environment.

Levels offered: Associate (limited number of programs), Bachelor's, Master's, Doctoral (limited number of programs).

Typical courses: Insects and Insect Control, Pesticide Laws and Regulations, Applied Entomology, Biological Control of Insects, Plant Pathology.

Related/complementary majors: aptitude for biological science, analytical ability, problem-solving skills.

Career possibilities: extension specialist, pest control technician or researcher, sales representative for pesticide companies.

Podiatry

Describes the anatomy, physiology, disorders, diseases, and acre and treatment of the foot.

Levels offered: Doctoral.

Typical courses: Basic Operative Podiatry, Functional Orthopedics, Peripheral Vascular Disease, Sports Medicine, Pediatric pathology.

Related/complementary majors: Anatomy, Pathology, Physiology.

Needed abilities: excellent aptitude for biology, chemistry, physics, analytical ability, problem-solving skills, excellent manual dexterity, good interpersonal skills.

Career possibilities: podiatrist.

Political Science and Government

Describes and analyzes political institutions and processes, including the origin, development, geographical units, forms, sources of authority, powers, purposes, functions, and operations of government.

Levels offered: Associate, Bachelor's, Master's, Doctoral.

Typical courses: United States Foreign Policy, Power in American Society, Minorities and Politics, Soviet Politics, Politics of American Economic Policy.

Related/complementary majors: History.

Needed abilities: excellent aptitude for the social sciences, analytical ability.

Career possibilities: diplomat, journalist, politician.

Polymer Engineering/Science

Describes the development and application of commercially viable polymer-related materials.

Levels offered: Bachelor's, Master's, Doctoral.

Typical courses: Polymer Concepts, Physical Properties of Polymers, Polymer Technology, Polymer Structure and Categorization.

Related/complementary majors: Chemistry, Physics, Materials Engineering.

Needed abilities: excellent aptitude for physical and chemical science, analytical ability.

Career possibilities: polymer engineering.

Popular Culture

Focuses on the impact of various aspects of our culture (such as television, popular music/books/magazines, sports, festivals, holidays, and folklore) on daily living and the values of society.

Levels offered: Bachelor's, Master's.

Typical courses: Contexts of Popular Music, Popular Culture and Media, Television as Popular Culture, Folktale and Legend, History of Popular Literature.

Related/complementary majors: Sociology, American Studies.

Needed abilities: aptitude for social science, analytical ability.

Career possibilities: media analyst, popular culture writer.

Poultry

Describes the theories, principles, and applications of appropriate technical skills that apply to the production and management of poultry and poultry products.

Levels offered: Associate, Bachelor's, Master's, Doctoral.

Typical courses: Poultry Production, Commercial Egg Production, Poultry Feeding, Poultry Diseases.

Related/complementary majors: Agriculture, Agricultural Business.

Needed abilities: aptitude for applied biological science, ability to apply business principles to the poultry industry, analytical ability, problem-solving skills.

Career possibilities: manager of a poultry farm, technician in a poultry processing plant, poultry scientist.

Printmaking

Describes the artistic production of various types of prints.

Levels offered: Bachelor's, Master's.

Typical courses: Woodcut/Linocut, Etching and Calligraphy, Screenprinting, Lithography.

Related/complementary majors: Drawing, Graphic Design, Illustration Design.

Needed abilities: eye for visual detail, creativity, manual dexterity.

Career possibilities: artist/printmaker.

Professional Sales and Sales Management

Develops sales process, sales management, and prospecting skills.

Levels offered: Bachelor's.

Typical courses: Professional Sales Process, Sales Management, Prospecting Methods, Sales Motivation and Performance.

Related/complementary majors: Business, Marketing.

Needed abilities: aptitude for business, good interpersonal and oral communication skills, persuasive ability.

Career possibilities: sales representative/manager.

Psychology, General

Describes the behavior and experience of people.

Levels offered: Associate, Bachelor's, Master's, Doctoral.

Typical courses: History of Psychology, Principles of behavior, Sensation and Perception, Abnormal Psychology, Psychological Statistics.

Related/complementary majors: Sociology.

Needed abilities: excellent aptitude for psychosocial science, analytical ability.

Career possibilities: human services worker, psychologist (with a graduate degree).

Psychometrics

Describes the mathematical and statistical procedures used in psychological test construction and validation.

Levels offered: Master's, Doctoral.

Typical courses: Intelligence Testing, Personality Testing, Multivariate Analysis, Advanced Clinical Assessment, Clinical Approaches to Children with Learning Disabilities.

Related/complementary majors: Education, Psychology, Statistics.

Needed abilities: strong aptitude for the social sciences and mathematics/statistics, analytical ability.

Career possibilities: test developer, psychologist.

Public Administration

Describes the knowledge, skills, values, and behaviors involved in the formulation of public policies and the management of public services.

Levels offered: Bachelor's (limited number of programs, Master's, Doctoral.

Typical courses: History of Public Administration, The Legislative Process, Decisions and Strategy Planning, Administration of Financial Resources, Personnel Administration.

Related/complementary majors: Business Administration and Management, Political Science and Government.

Needed abilities: aptitude for business, economics, legal issues, and social sciences, managerial ability, analytical ability, problem-solving skills.

Career possibilities: government official, manager of a public agency.

Public Health

Describes the techniques and procedures for developing and providing public preventative and curative health services.

Levels offered: Bachelor's (limited number of programs), Master's, Doctoral.

Typical courses: Issues in Health Planning, Viral Diseases, Community Health Education, Clinical Epidemiology, Community Mental Health.

Complementary/related majors: Biostatistics, Epidemiology, Health Education.

Needed abilities: aptitude for the behavioral, social, and biomedical sciences, analytical ability, problem-solving skills.

Career possibilities: administrator of a health care program or service, health educator or planner.

Public Relations

Describes the methods and techniques by which the public can be induced to have understanding of and good will towards a person, firm, or institution.

Levels offered: Bachelor's, Master's, Doctoral.

Typical courses: Business Communication, Persuasion, Communications Law, Representing Interest Groups, Writing for Television and Radio.

Related/complementary majors: Advertising, Marketing.

Needed abilities: excellent oral and written communication skills, analytical ability, problem-solving skills, creativity, good interpersonal skills, aptitude for applied psychology.

Career possibilities: publicist, public relations manager.

Pure Mathematics

Describes number, form, arrangement, and associated relationships using rigorously defined literal numerical and operational symbols.

Levels offered: Bachelor's, Master's, Doctoral.

Typical courses: Differential Equations, Symbolic Logic< Linear Algebra, Differential Geometry, Topics in Real Analysis.

Related/complementary majors: Mathematics, General.

Needed abilities: excellent aptitude for mathematics and logical thinking, analytical ability, problem-solving skills.

Career possibilities: mathematician.

Quality Control

Prepares individuals to support engineers or managers by utilizing the sciences of measurement and quality control, quality design, production and inspection, testing, statistical sampling, and mathematical probability as it relates to quality control in mass-produced items manufactured by modern production procedures and processes.

Levels offered: Associate, Bachelor's, Master's.

Typical courses: Statistical Techniques for Quality Control, Measurements for Quality Control, Procurement Quality Control, Reliability-Quality Control Engineering.

Related/complementary majors: Industrial Technology, Manufacturing Technology.

Needed abilities: good ability for applied physics and mathematics, analytical ability, problem-solving skills, orientation to detail, ability to work accurately and precisely under the direction of an engineer or manager.

Career possibilities: quality control technician or manager, engineering assistant, production assistant.

Quantitative Psychology

Describes the application of mathematical and statistical models and methodology in psychology.

Levels offered: Bachelor's, Master's.

Typical courses: Quantitative Aspects of Measurement, Survey Research in Psychology, Matrices and Differential Equations, Advanced Design and Statistics.

Related/complementary majors: Psychometrics, Statistics.

Needed abilities: excellent aptitude for psychology and mathematics, analytical ability, problem-solving skills.

Career possibilities: psychological researcher, psychological test developer.

Radiologic Technology

Prepares individuals to apply roentgen rays and radioactive substances to patients for diagnostic and therapeutic purposes, under the supervision of a radiologist.

Levels offered: Associate, Bachelor's, Master's.

Typical courses: Radiographic Anatomy and Positioning, Computers in Radiologic Science, Radiographic Techniques, Elementary Radiation Protection, Radiological Physics.

Related/complementary majors: Anatomy, Biophysics, Physics, Physiology, Ultrasound Technology, Nuclear Medicine.

Needed abilities: aptitude for applied physics and biology, good interpersonal skills, orientation to detail, ability to work under the direction of a physician.

Career possibilities: radiologic technician.

Range Management

Describes the principles and practices involved in determining and applying uses of range resources to ensure sustained productivity and resource conservation.

Levels offered: Bachelor's, Master's (limited number pf programs).

Typical courses: Range Resource Economics, Wildland Ecosystems, Rangeland Appraisal, Range Vegetation Analysis, Grassland Desert Range Plans.

Related/complementary majors: Agronomy, Ecology, Wildlife Management, Conservation Biology.

Needed abilities: aptitude for natural science, analytical ability, problem-solving skills.

Career possibilities: conservation officer, ecologist, park naturalist, game farm manager.

Reading Education

Describes the theories, methods, and techniques of designing, implementing, and evaluating of programs which prepare, upgrade, or retrain students in learning.

Levels offered: Bachelor's, Master's, Doctoral.

Typical courses: Language Development and Reading, Cognitive Bases of Reading, Reading in the Content Area, Microcomputers in Reading, Diagnostic and Corrective Reading Instruction.

Related/complementary majors: Curriculum and Instruction, Education.

Needed abilities: excellent interpersonal and communication skills, analytical ability, problem-solving skills.

Career possibilities: reading teacher.

Real Estate

Describes the theories and techniques of buying, selling, appraising, renting, managing, and leasing of real property.

Levels offered: Associate (limited number of programs), Bachelor's, Master's, Doctoral (limited number of programs).

Typical courses: Real Estate Principles and Practices, Real Estate Law, Real Estate Finance, Real Estate Appraising, Real Estate Fundamentals.

Related/complementary majors: Business Administration and Management.

Needed abilities: aptitude for business, analytical ability.

Career possibilities: real estate appraiser, real estate developer, real estate broker.

Recreational Therapy

Prepares individuals to plan, organize, and direct recreation activities such as sports, trips, dramatics, and crafts to help clients in recovering from illness or in coping with a disability.

Levels offered: Associate, Bachelor's, Master's, Doctoral.

Typical courses: Physical Activities for the Mentally/Emotionally Disabled, Leisure Counseling, Swim Instruction for the Disabled, Camp Counseling, Fundraising and Volunteerism.

Related/complementary majors: Dance Therapy, Music Therapy, Occupational Therapy.

Career possibilities: recreational therapist, activities director.

Rehabilitation Counseling

Prepares individuals to help people with disabilities obtain gainful employment.

Levels offered: Bachelor's, Master's, Doctoral.

Typical courses: Job Placement in the Rehabilitation Process, Medical Aspects of Disability, Work Evaluation, The Industrially Injured Worker, Human Interaction in Rehabilitation.

Related/complementary majors: Occupational Therapy, Psychology, Social Work.

Needed abilities: excellent interpersonal skills, aptitude for behavioral and social sciences, analytical ability, problem-solving skills, ability to understand medical and psychological problems and terminology.

Career possibilities: employee assistance counselor, rehabilitation counselor, insurance adjuster.

Religion

Describes the origin, histories, organized forms, beliefs, worship, and practices of religions.

Levels offered: Associate, Bachelor's, Master's, Doctoral.

Typical courses: Belief and Unbelief, Religion in America, Introduction to the Bible, Religious Ethics, World Religions.

Related/complementary majors: Bible Studies, Religious Education, Theological Studies.

Needed abilities: aptitude for social science and theology, analytical ability.

Career possibilities: religious educator, religious writer.

Religious Education

Describes the theories, methods, and techniques of designing and implementing activities for religious education.

Levels offered: Bachelor's, Master's, Doctoral.

Typical courses: Methods and Curriculum in Religious Education, Christian Education, Understanding the Bible, Leadership Training and Supervision, Religious Education Practicum.

Related/complementary majors: Education, Missionary Studies, Religion.

Needed abilities: excellent communication skills, aptitude for religious philosophy and practice.

Career possibilities: religious educator, religious writer.

Respiratory Therapy

Prepares individuals to administer respiratory care under the direction of a physician, evaluating the patient's progress, and making recommendations for respiratory therapy.

Levels offered: Associate, Bachelor's.

Typical courses: Medical Gas Therapeutics, Pathophysiology of Pulmonary Disease, Respiratory Care of the Medical/Surgical

Patient, Pulmonary Rehabilitation and Home Care, Pulmonary Function Testing.

Related/complementary majors: Biochemistry, Biology, Chemistry, Exercise Physiology, Physiology.

Needed abilities: excellent aptitude for the physical, chemical, and biological sciences, good interpersonal skills, orientation to details, analytical ability, problem-solving skills, ability to use complex machinery.

Career possibilities: respiratory therapist.

Retailing

Prepares individuals to apply marketing skills in retail establishments.

Levels offered: Associate, Bachelor's, Master's.

Typical courses: Merchandising Seminar, Fashion Show Procedures, Consumer Behavior, Merchandising Display.

Related/complementary majors: Business Management, Fashion Merchandising, Small Business Management and Ownership.

Needed abilities: aptitude for business and applies psychology, problem-solving skills.

Career possibilities: buyer, sales manager.

Rhetoric

Describes the effective use of language, including an examination of the patterned use of language for its effects.

Levels offered: Bachelor's, Master's, Doctoral.

Typical courses: Advanced Argumentative Writing, American Political Rhetoric, Rhetoric of Drama, Rhetorical Theory and Oral Argument, Rhetoric of Legal Theory.

Related/complementary majors: Advertising, Linguistics, Psychology, Public Relations, Speech.

Needed abilities: excellent communication skills (written and oral), aptitude for applied psychology and language, analytical ability.

Career possibilities: advertising copywriter, public relations worker, speech writer.

Russian and East European Studies

Describes the history, society, politics, culture, and economics of Russia and East European countries.

Levels offered: Bachelor's, Master's, Doctoral.

Typical courses: Economic Theory and Development in Communist Countries, Russian Literature, The Soviet Union and Europe, Russian and Soviet Thought, Governments and Politics of Eastern Europe.

Related/complementary majors: Anthropology, Art History and Appreciation, Comparative Literature, Economics, History, International Business, International Studies, Music History and Appreciation, Political Science and Government, Sociology.

Needed abilities: aptitude for all aspects of social science, analytical ability.

Career possibilities: diplomat, Soviet affairs analyst/writer, international businessperson.

Scandinavian Studies

Describes the history, society, politics, culture, and economics of Scandinavia, including Denmark, Norway, Sweden, and Finland.

Levels offered: Bachelor's, Master's, Doctoral.

Typical courses: Scandinavian Mythology and Folklore, Finland: East and West, Modern Scandinavian Society, Hans Christian Andersen and His World, Scandinavian Life and Culture.

Related/complementary majors: Anthropology, Art History and Appreciation, Comparative Literature, Economics, History, International Business, International Business, Music History and Appreciation, Political Science and Government, Sociology.

Career possibilities: diplomat, international businessperson.

School Counseling

Prepares individuals to provide counseling services to students in elementary through high school.

Levels offered: Master's.

Typical courses: School Counseling Theories, Ethics and Legal Issues in School Counseling, Introduction to Group Counseling in

Schools, Play Methods in School Counseling, Substance Abuse Prevention/Intervention in Schools.

Related/complementary majors: Counseling.

Needed abilities: excellent interpersonal and communication skills, analytical ability, problem-solving skills.

Career possibilities: school counselor.

School Psychology

Describes the study, selection, and application of methods, facts, and theories of psychology that relate to individual learning in formal educational courses.

Levels offered: Master's, Doctoral.

Typical courses: Psychological Tests and Measurements, Principles and Practices of Intelligence Testing, Statistics in Education, Educational Diagnosis for the School Psychologist, Cognitive Function Models for Prescriptive Educational Planning.

Related/complementary major: Education, Psychometrics, Educational Psychology.

Needed abilities: excellent aptitude for social science, excellent communication skills, analytical ability, problem-solving skills.

Career possibilities: school psychologist.

Science Education

Describes the theories, methods, and techniques involved in teaching the subject matter of life sciences, natural sciences, and physical sciences.

Levels offered: Bachelor's, Master's, Doctoral.

Typical courses: Science Curriculum Improvement, Science, Technology, and Education, Seminar in Environmental Sciences, Computer Based Instruction for Secondary Science Programs, Chemistry Curriculum and Methods Laboratory.

Related/complementary majors: Biology, Chemistry, Education, Physics.

Needed abilities: excellent interpersonal and communication skills, excellent aptitude for science, analytical ability, problem-solving skills.

Career possibilities: science teacher.

137

Sculpture

Describes the aesthetic qualities, techniques, and creative processes for creating works of art in three dimensions through carving, molding, welding, or other procedures.

Levels offered: Bachelor's, Master's.

Typical courses: Metal Technique, Wax Sculpting for Casting, Figure Modeling, History of Sculpture, Line, Light, Shadow, and the Object.

Related/complementary majors: Art History and Appreciation, Ceramics, Metals.

Needed abilities: eye for artistic detail, manual dexterity, creativity.

Sign Language Interpreting

Prepares individuals to interpret for the hearing impaired.

Levels offered: Associate, Bachelor's (limited number of programs).

Typical courses: Principles of American Sign Language for Interpreters, Finger Spelling and Number Comprehension, Expressive Transliteration, Principles of Note-taking/Tutoring, Voice Interpreting.

Related/complementary majors: Education of the Hearing Impaired.

Needed abilities: proficiency in sign language, excellent communication and interpersonal skills.

Career possibilities: interpreter for the deaf.

Small Business Management and Ownership

Describes management functions, policies, and procedures that are characteristic of small business concerns.

Levels offered: Associate, Bachelor's.

Typical courses: Legal Aspects of Small Business, Records Management, Contracts and Sales, Business Financing, Public Relations Principles.

Related/complementary majors: Entrepreneurship.

Needed abilities: analytical abilities, strong problem-solving skills, versatility and capability for varied managerial tasks.

Career possibilities: small business manager/owner.

Social Psychology

Describes the behavior of the individual as a member of a group, and the processes of associating individuals together.

Levels offered: Master's, Doctoral.

Typical courses: Group Behavior, Social Cognition, Experimental Methods in Social Psychology, Attitude Formation and Change, Interpersonal Influence, Social Power, and Health.

Related/complementary majors: Sociology, Industrial and Organizational Psychology.

Needed abilities: excellent aptitude for psychosocial science, analytical ability.

Career possibilities: psychological researcher/writer.

Social Studies Education

Describes the theories, methods, and techniques involved in teaching the subject matter of social studies.

Levels offered: Bachelor's, Master's, Doctoral.

Typical courses: Microcomputers in Social Studies, Social Studies Curriculum Methods, Problems and Developments in Secondary School Social Studies, Urban Ecological Problems and Curriculum.

Related/complementary majors: Geography, History, Political Science and Government.

Needed abilities: excellent interpersonal and communication skills, excellent aptitude for social studies, analytical ability.

Career possibilities: social studies teacher.

Social Work

Describes the social interventions that enhance, conserve, and augment the means by which persons, individually or collectively, can solve disruptions in their social existence.

Levels offered: Bachelor's, Master's, Doctoral.

Typical courses: Social Planning and Administrative Processes, Social Policy: Family and Children, Community Practice in Mental Health Settings, Human Behavior and the Social Environment, Human Development, Illness, and Disability.

Related/complementary majors: Marriage and Family Counseling, Sociology.

Needed abilities: excellent interpersonal skills, aptitude for behavioral and social sciences, analytical ability, problem-solving skills.

Career possibilities: social worker, administrator of a social service agency, counselor.

Sociology

Describes the human society, social institutions, and social relationships, including the development, purposes, structures, and functions of human groups.

Levels offered: Associate, Bachelor's, Master's, Doctoral.

Typical courses: Social Stratification, The Urban Community, Complex Organizations, Sociology of Aging, Sociology of Women.

Related/complementary majors: Anthropology, Area and Ethnic Studies, Popular Culture, Psychology, Urban Studies, Women's Studies.

Needed abilities: excellent aptitude for social sciences, analytical ability.

Career possibilities: social analyst, researcher.

Software Engineering

Trains individuals to develop complex, large-scale software systems.

Levels offered: Bachelor's, Master's, Doctoral.

Typical courses: Operating System Architecture, Computer Systems for Software Engineers, Usability and Design, C++ Programming.

Related/complementary majors: Computer Science, Electronics Engineering.

Needed abilities: good ability for math and applied computer science, analytical ability, problem-solving skills, creativity.

Career possibilities: software developer/designer/tester.

Soil Sciences

Describes the physical, chemical, and biological sciences and basic principles that relate to the determination of soil properties and their conservation and management for crop production and other purposes.

Levels offered: Associate, Bachelor's, Master's, Doctoral.

Typical courses: Soil and Water Chemistry, Soil and Plant Nutrition, Irrigated Soils, Fertilizer Technology, Soil Identification and Interpretations.

Related/complementary majors: Agronomy.

Needed abilities: excellent aptitude for biological, chemical, and physical sciences, analytical ability, problem-solving skills.

Career possibilities: social conservationist/scientist/technician.

Special Education, General

Describes the theories, methods, and techniques of designing, implementing, and evaluating organized learning activities for students whose physical, emotional, cognitive, or social needs require a special curriculum and educational setting.

Levels offered: Bachelor's, Master's, Doctoral.

Typical courses: Career Education for the Exceptional Individual, Teaching Exceptional Individuals, Language Development and the Exceptional Individual, Educational Diagnosis of the Exceptional Individual, Survey of Special Education.

Related/complementary majors: other Education majors, Psychology.

Needed abilities: excellent interpersonal and communication skills, analytical ability, problem-solving skills.

Career possibilities: special educator.

Specific Learning Disabilities

Describes the theories, methods, and techniques of designing, implementing, and evaluating organized learning activities for students whose perception, communication, or motor skills require a special curriculum and educational setting.

Levels offered: Bachelor's, Master's, Doctoral.

Typical courses: Diagnosis and Assessment in Learning Disabilities, Curriculum Practices for Children with Learning Disabilities, Language and Reading Disorders, Practicum, Learning Styles.

Related/complementary majors: other Education majors, Psychology.

Needed abilities: excellent interpersonal and communication skills, analytical ability, problem-solving skills.

Career possibilities: teacher of the learning disabled.

Speech, Debate, and Forensics

Describes the theory, methods, and skills needed for improving competence in speaking and listening and the application of forms of argument to testing ideas or making decisions.

Levels offered: Bachelor's, Master's, Doctoral.

Typical courses: Interpersonal Communication, Oral Interpretation, Argumentation and Debate, Business and Professional Speaking, Voice and Diction.

Related/complementary majors: English, Rhetoric.

Needed abilities: excellent oral communication skills, analytical ability.

Career possibilities: public speaker, speechwriter, television commentator.

Speech-Language Pathology

Prepares individuals to evaluate and habilitate speech and language disorders such as neurological disturbances, defective articulation, or foreign dialect in children and adults.

Levels offered: Master's, Doctoral.

Typical courses: Augmentative Communication, Audiology, Stuttering, Structure and Function of the Speaking Mechanism.

Related/complementary majors: Audiology, Communication Science and Disorders.

Needed abilities: aptitude for anatomy and physiology, analytical ability, problem-solving skills, excellent communication skills.

Career possibilities: speech/language therapist.

Sports Management

Describes the marketing and management of sports and related recreational activities.

Levels offered: Associate, Bachelor's, Master's.

Typical courses: Sport Facility Design and Management, Economics of Sport, Sport Marketing, Budgeting and Financing of Sport, Sports Administration Internship.

Related/complementary majors: Sports Studies, Recreation, Business.

Needed abilities: aptitude for marketing and management.

Career possibilities: sport manager, sport promoter.

Sports Medicine

Prepares individuals to prevent, evaluate, and treat athletic injuries.

Levels offered: Bachelor's, Master's.

Typical courses: Prevention and Treatment of Athletic Injuries, Scientific Principles of Athletic Conditioning, Techniques of Advanced Exercise Testing, Theory of Weight Training.

Related/complementary majors: Anatomy, Exercise Physiology, Physical Therapy, Physiology, Physical Education.

Needed abilities: aptitude for applied biomedical science, analytical ability, problem-solving skills, good interpersonal skills, physical stamina, manual dexterity.

Career possibilities: sports medicine practitioner/sports trainer.

Sports Psychology

Prepares individuals to apply psychological principles and practices to maximize the performance of athletes.

Levels offered: Master's, Doctoral.

Typical courses: Ethics in Sports Psychology, Psychology of Coaching, Optimum Sport Performance, Sport Medicine and the Psychology of Injury, Psychophysiology of Human Motor Activity.

Related/complementary majors: Counseling Psychology, Sports Medicine.

Needed abilities: strong aptitude for psychosocial science and physiology, appreciation of sport, analytical ability, problem-solving skills, good interpersonal skills.

Career possibilities: sports psychologist, personal trainer, coach.

Sports Studies

Describes all issues relating to sports.

Levels offered: Bachelor's, Master's, Doctoral.

Typical courses: Sport Marketing, History of Sport, Sport and the Law, Social Psychology of Sport, Sport Business and Finance.

Related/complementary majors: Business Administration and Management, Psychology, Sociology.

Needed abilities: aptitude for social science and business, analytical ability.

Career possibilities: sports commentator or writer.

Statistics

Describes the probabilistic models involving a finite number of outcomes and the science of collecting, describing, and interpreting numerical data.

Levels offered: Bachelor's, Master's, Doctoral.

Typical courses: Applied Time Series, Advanced Theory of Survey Sampling, Measure Theory and Probability, Nonparametric Statistical Methods, Applied Business Statistics.

Related/complementary majors: Mathematics.

Needed abilities: excellent aptitude for mathematics, analytical ability, logical and reasoning ability.

Career possibilities: statistician, researcher.

Structural Engineering

Prepares students for engineering careers with focus on construction materials and structural systems.

Levels offered: Bachelor's, Master's, Doctoral.

Typical courses: Wood Structures, Concrete Structures, Steel Structures, Structural Analysis, Theory of Elasticity.

Related/complementary majors: Civil Engineering, Construction.

Needed abilities: excellent aptitude for chemistry, physics, and mathematics, analytical ability, problem-solving skills.

Career possibilities: structural engineer.

Student Personnel Services

Develops administrators for college and university services such as admissions, student housing, disability support, financial aid, counseling, and recreation.

Levels offered: Master's, Doctoral.

Typical courses: Administration of College Personnel Services, College Student Athletes, Using Tests in Counseling, Trends in Career Development, History and Philosophy of Higher Education.

Related/complementary majors: Psychology, Social Work, Counseling, Higher Education Administration.

Needed abilities: aptitude for applied psychosocial science, excellent interpersonal skills, analytical ability, problem-solving skills.

Career possibilities: financial aid officer, admissions representative, student housing director, career services coordinator.

Surgical Technology

Prepares individuals to serve as general technical assistants before, during, and after surgical operations.

Levels offered: Associate.

Typical courses: Anatomy and Physiology, Medical Terminology, Surgical Specialties, Surgical Procedures.

Related/complementary majors: Nursing, Medical Assisting.

Needed abilities: aptitude for basic biological science, good manual dexterity, ability to work under pressure, orientation to detail, ability to work according to precise standards established by a surgeon.

Career possibilities: surgical technician.

Surveying and Mapping Sciences

Describes the determination and identification of the shape, contour, location, and dimensions of land or water and their features.

Levels offered: Bachelor's, Master's, Doctoral.

Typical courses: Conformal Map Projections, Principles and Techniques of Remote Sensing, Electronic and Satellite Surveying, General Photogrammetry and Photo-Interpreting, Subdivision Design and Layout.

Related/complementary majors: Geography.

Needed abilities: aptitude for physical science and mathematics, analytical ability, excellent spatial perception and orientation to visual details.

Career possibilities: cartographer, surveyor.

Surveying and Mapping Technology

Prepares individuals to assist surveyors, cartographers, civil engineers and urban planners in the determination and description of the shape, contour, location, and dimensions of geographic areas or features.

Levels offered: Associate.

Typical courses: Surveying Field Practice, Land Surveying, Construction Surveying, Technical Computations, Cartography.

Related/complementary majors: Geography.

Needed abilities: aptitude for physical science and mathematics, orientation to visual details, ability to work precisely.

Career possibilities: surveying or mapping assistant.

Systems Engineering

Describes the interacting, interrelated, or interdependent elements forming the related engineering systems.

Levels offered: Bachelor's, Master's, Doctoral.

Typical courses: Digital Systems Simulation, Industrial Ergonomics, Deterministic Control Systems, Production Systems Analysis, Human Interaction with Computers and Software.

Related majors: Engineering Science.

Needed abilities: excellent aptitude for physics and mathematics, analytical ability, problem-solving skills.

Career possibilities: systems engineer.

Taxation

Describes the principles, procedures, and regulations applicable to the maintenance of records and the preparation and filing of income tax returns for individuals, partnerships, corporations, and other types of organizations.

Levels offered: Master's.

Typical courses: State and Local Taxation, Estate and Gift Taxation, Corporate Taxation, International Tax Practice, Federal Taxation of Income.

Related/complementary majors: Accounting, Investments and Securities, Law.

Needed abilities: aptitude for business and mathematics, analytical ability.

Career possibilities: investment advisor, tax consultant.

Teaching English as a Second Language

Describes the theories, methods, and techniques of designing, implementing, and evaluating organized learning activities for students whose native language is not English.

Levels offered: Bachelor's, Master's.

Typical courses: Principles of Bilingual Education, Practicum in Teaching English as a Second Language, Development of Communication Skills in Limited English Proficiency Students, Teaching the Structure of the English Language to Limited English Proficiency Students.

Related/complementary majors: Bilingual/Bicultural Education, Education, English, Linguistics.

Needed abilities: excellent communication skills, analytical ability, problem-solving skills.

Career possibilities: teacher of English as a second language.

Technical and Business Writing/ Communications

Focuses on the theory, methods, and skills needed for scientific, technical, and business papers.

Levels offered: Bachelor's, Master's.

Typical courses: Technical Editing, Writing Software User Manuals, Public Relations, Advanced Composition, Advanced Business Communications.

Related/complementary majors: Business, Journalism, English, Science.

Needed abilities: excellent writing skills, ability to understand and communicate information about business, science, or technology.

Career possibilities: technical or business writer/editor, publications director, grant/proposal writer.

Technology Education

Prepares individuals to teach trade and industrial courses.

Levels offered: Bachelor's, Master's.

Typical courses: Energy and Power Systems, Manufacturing and Transportation, Technological Design, Information and Communication Technology Lab, Instructional Methods for Middle School Technology Education.

Related/complementary majors: Carpentry, Drafting and Design Education, Secondary Education. Graphics Technology, Welding, Computer majors, Auto Technology.

Needed abilities: excellent interpersonal and communication skills, aptitude for technology and industrial subjects, analytical ability, problem-solving skills.

Career possibilities: technology teacher.

Television/Radio/Film Production

Levels offered: Associate, Bachelor's, Master's.

Typical courses: Fundamentals of Cinematic Sound, Motion Picture Editing, Radio Workshop, Introduction to Art Direction, Television Documentary Production.

Related/complementary courses: Entertainment Technology.

Needed abilities: creativity, analytical ability, problem-solving skills.

Career possibilities: film/television/radio writer, director, technician, producer.

Textile Engineering

Describes the structure, reactions, functions, properties, and synthesis of textiles.

Levels offered: Bachelor's, Master's, Doctoral.

Typical courses: Textile Finishes, Dyeing Theory, Structures of Fibers and Polymers, Advanced Mechanics of Flexible Structures, Carpet Manufacturing.

Related/complementary majors: Physical Chemistry, Industrial Engineering, Physics.

Needed abilities: excellent aptitude for chemistry, physics, and mathematics, analytical ability, problem-solving skills.

Career possibilities: textile engineer.

Textile Technology

Prepares individuals to assist scientists, engineers, or managers in textile research, development, production, or servicing.

Levels offered: Associate, Bachelor's.

Typical courses: Textile Quality Control, Texturized Yarns, Dyeing and Finishing of Textile Materials, Analytical Instrumentation in Textiles, Plant Operation and Cost Control.

Related/complementary majors: Industrial Technology, Manufacturing Technology, Textiles and Clothing.

Needed abilities: aptitude for applied science and technology, analytical ability, problem-solving skills.

Career possibilities: textile technician.

Textiles and Clothing

Describes the ways of meeting psychological, sociological, economic, and physiological needs for clothing and textiles, including techniques of production, distribution, marketing, consumption, refurbishing, and relevant legislation.

Levels offered: Associate, Bachelor's, Master's, Doctoral.

Typical courses: Apparel Production Management, Consumer and Applied Textiles, History of Textiles, Textile Testing, Family Clothing Consumption.

Related/complementary majors: Business Administration and Management, Fashion Design, Fashion Merchandising, Fibers/Textiles/Weaving.

Needed abilities: aptitude for business and social science, analytical ability, problem-solving skills.

Theatre Design

Describes the techniques of communicating information, ideas, moods, and feelings through set design and costuming with attention to both function and aesthetics.

Levels offered: Associate, Bachelor's, Master's.

Typical courses: Stagecraft, Set Design, Lighting Design, Scene Painting, Costume Design.

Related/complementary majors: Film, Dramatic Arts, Fashion Design.

Needed abilities: eye for artistic detail, creativity, moderate mechanical/technical aptitude.

Career possibilities: set designer, lighting designer, costume designer.

Theological Professions

Prepares individuals to become priests, ministers, rabbis, and other technological professionals.

Levels offered: Doctoral.

Typical courses: Integration of Theology and Practice, Expository Teaching, Pastoral Psychology, Theory and Practice of Ministry, Society, Religion, and Ethics.

Related/complementary majors: Bible Studies, Religion Theological Studies, Religious Education.

Needed abilities: excellent aptitude for understanding and applying religious thoughts and practices, excellent interpersonal and communication skills.

Career possibilities: priest, rabbi, minister.

Theological Studies

Describes the history and evolution of religious beliefs relating to a divine being.

Levels offered: Associate, Bachelor's, Master's, Doctoral.

Typical courses: Medieval Theology, Post-Reformation Theology, Roman Catholic Theology, Evangelism, The Theology of Paul.

Related/complementary majors: Bible Studies, Religion.

Needed abilities: good aptitude for religious philosophy and history, analytical ability.

Career possibilities: religious educator, religious writer.

Toxicology

Describes the nature, source, identification, and characteristics of poisons, toxic substances, and exogenous chemical agents which can cause death, illness, or injury upon contact with, or ingestion into the body.

Levels offered: Master's, Doctoral.

Typical courses: Analytical Toxicology, Biochemical Toxicology, Poison Control, Antidotes, Forensic Toxicology.

Related/complementary majors: Biochemistry, Forensic Science/Studies.

Needed abilities: excellent aptitude for biological and chemical sciences, analytical ability.

Career possibilities: toxicologist.

Transportation Management

Describes the nature and application of management methods and techniques related to transportation enterprises.

Levels offered: Associate, Bachelor's, Master's.

Typical courses: Economics of Transportation Management, Decision Theory, Transportation Analysis, Transportation Policy, Urban Transport Economics.

Related/complementary majors: Business Administration and Management, Public Administration, Urban Design, Urban Planning.

Needed abilities: aptitude for business, analytical ability, problem-solving skills.

Career possibilities: transportation analyst/manager/consultant.

Travel and Tourism

Prepares individuals to perform marketing and management functions and tasks in enterprises engaged in passenger transportation, travel services, and tourism.

Levels offered: Associate, Bachelor's, Master's.

Typical courses: Introduction to Travel and Tourism, Management of Group Travel, Computer Systems, Conference and Convention Planning, Management of Tourism Agencies.

Related/complementary majors: Business Administration and Management.

Needed abilities: aptitude for business, good interpersonal skills, planning and organizational skills, orientation to details, problem-solving skills.

Career possibilities: convention manager, tourism director, travel agent.

Urban and Regional Planning

Describes the application of the planning process to the development of environmental programs design to deal with urban, regional, and other geographical distinct areas.

Levels offered: Bachelor's, Master's, Doctoral.

Typical courses: Environmental Impact Assessment. Land Development Controls, Transportation Planning, Planning for Housing, Planning for Historic Preservation.

Related/complementary majors: Urban Design/Studies, Public Administration, Historic Preservation.

Needed abilities: aptitude for social science and management science, analytical ability, problem-solving skills.

Career possibilities: city/community planner, consultant, public administrator.

Urban Design

Describes the systematic process of creating and modifying those physical elements which constitute a city, synthesizing function, aesthetic sensitivity, technology, and social, psychological, and economic well-being.

Levels offered: Master's, Doctoral.

Typical courses: Cities of Tomorrow, Urban Analysis, Housing Problems, Theory of City Form, Methods of Downtown Development.

Related/complementary majors: Architecture, Environmental Design, Urban Studies, Urban and Regional Planning.

Needed abilities: aptitude for applied psychology, economics, and technology, analytical ability, problem-solving skills, creativity, eye for visual detail.

Career possibilities: developer, site planner, urban designer/planner.

Urban Studies

Describes the history, society, politics, culture, and economics of urban areas.

Levels offered: Bachelor's, Master's, Doctoral.

Typical courses: Urban Crime Patterns, Urban Transportation,

Minority Cultures, Housing and Community Revitalization, History of Urban Development.

Related/complementary majors: Urban and Regional Planning, Criminology, Economics, Ethic Studies, History, Political Science, Public Administration, Sociology, Urban Design.

Needed abilities: excellent aptitude for sociology, history, political science, and economics, analytical ability, problem-solving skills.

Career possibilities: city government manager, writer of urban issues.

Veterinary Technology

Prepares individuals to assist a veterinary doctor in providing care and treatment to animals.

Levels offered: Associate.

Typical courses: veterinary Anatomy and Physiology, Preventative Medicine and Immunology, Pet and Lab Animal Science, Pharmacology.

Related/complementary majors: Zoology.

Needed abilities: good aptitude for biological science, animal handling ability, ability to work according to established standards and to follow procedures designated by a veterinary doctor.

Career possibilities: animal caretaker and handler, veterinary technician or assistant.

Veterinary Medicine

Describes the nature, prevention, and treatment of animal diseases.

Levels offered: Doctoral.

Typical courses: Small Medicine, Equine Surgery, Diagnostic Laboratory, Animal Reproduction, Veterinary Microbiology.

Related/complementary majors: Zoology.

Needed abilities: excellent aptitude for biological science, good animal handling ability, strong analytical ability, excellent problem-solving skills, good manual dexterity.

Career possibilities: veterinarian.

Video

Describes the aesthetic qualities, theories, techniques, and creative processes of the moving image using videotape as the medium.

Levels offered: Associate, Bachelor's, Master's.

Typical courses: Production Planning, Editing, Graphics, Special Effects, Practicum in Sound.

Related/complementary majors: Film.

Needed abilities: eye for visual detail, analytical ability, problem-solving skills, creativity.

Career possibilities: video director, producer, or technician.

Water and Wastewater Technology

Prepares individuals to process, purify, store, control pollution in, distribute, and dispose of wastewater.

Levels offered: Associate.

Typical courses: Sewage System Maintenance, Small Treatment Plants, Hydraulics of Water, Water Chemistry and Bacteriology, Water Systems Instrumentation and Controls.

Related/complementary majors: Chemistry, Physics, Civil Engineering Technology.

Needed abilities: aptitude for applied physics and chemistry, analytical ability, problem solving skills.

Career possibilities: water/wastewater technician.

Water Resources

Describes the analysis and management of water resources, including principles and techniques to ensure optimum yield, use, and conservation.

Levels offered: Bachelor's, Master's, Doctoral.

Typical courses: Groundwater Motion, Hydrogeology, Fluid Mechanics, Hydrology, Water Conservation.

Related/complementary majors: Environmental Engineering, Water and Wastewater Technology, Public Administration

Needed abilities: aptitude for natural science, analytical ability, problem-solving skills.

Career possibilities: water resource manager or director, water technologist.

Welding Technology

Prepares skilled workers at the technician level to understand, perform, supervise, and inspect a wide variety of welding procedures.

Levels offered: Associate.

Typical courses: Fundamentals of TIG and MIG Welding, Welding Fabrication, Design, and Testing, Metallurgy, Basic Arc Welding, Blueprint Reading.

Related/complementary majors: Construction.

Needed abilities: excellent visual perception, excellent manual dexterity, aptitude for basic technical mathematics, physical stamina.

Career possibilities: welder.

Wildlife Management

Prepares individuals in the principles and practices used in the production and improvement of wildlife.

Levels offered: Associate, Bachelor's, Master's, Doctoral.

Typical courses: Wildlife Economics, Wildlife Diseases, Wildlife Population Statistics, Management of Wildlife Habitat, Wildlife and Society: Contemporary Issues.

Related/complementary majors: Conservation Biology, Ecology, Zoology.

Needed abilities: aptitude for environmental and zoological science, analytical ability, problem-solving skills, managerial ability.

Career possibilities: wildlife manager or technician.

Women's Studies

Describes the history, society, politics, culture, and economics of women.

Levels offered: Bachelor's, Master's, Doctoral.

Typical courses: Women, Work, and Culture, Image of Women in African Art, Women, War, and Peace, Women in Music, Women's Health.

Related/complementary majors: Anthropology, Art History and Appreciation, History, Music History and Appreciation, Political Science, Psychology, Sociology.

Needed abilities: aptitude for social studies and science and the arts, analytical ability.

Career possibilities: educator, writer, director of programs and businesses for women.

Zoology

Describes animals, including their structure, function, reproduction, growth, heredity, evolution, behavior, and distribution.

Levels offered: Bachelor's, Master's, Doctoral.

Typical courses: Field Vertebrae Zoology, Embryology, Advanced Animal Behavior, Reproduction, Mammalian Physiology.

Related/complementary majors: Biology.

Needed abilities: excellent aptitude for biological science, analytical ability.

Career possibilities: animal caretaker, lab assistant, researcher.

Appendix I.
Major Fields of Study
by Discipline

Agriculture

Agribusiness and Agricultural Production
  Agricultural Business and
    Management
  Agricultural Economics
  Agricultural Mechanization/
    Technology
  Equestrian Studies
  Equine Business Manage-
    ment
  Horticulture
  International Agriculture

Agricultural Sciences
  Agriculture
  Agronomy
  Animal Sciences
  Dairy
  Equine Science
  Food Sciences
  Horticultural Science
  Plant Protection
  Poultry
  Range Management
  Soil Sciences

Renewable Natural Resources
  Fishing and Fisheries
  Forestry
  Forestry Production and Process-
    ing
  Water Resources
  Wildlife Management

Architecture and Environmental Design

Architecture
Architectural Technology
Environmental Design
Historic Preservation
Interior Design
Landscape Architecture
Urban Design
Urban and Regional Planning

Area and Ethnic Studies

African Studies
American Studies
Asian Studies
Latin American Studies
Middle Eastern Studies
Russian and East European Studies

Scandinavian Studies
Ethnic Studies
    African-American Studies
    American Indian/Native American Studies
    Jewish Studies

Business

Business and Management
    Accounting
    Aviation Management
    Banking and Financial Services
    Business Administration and Management
    Business Economics
    Entrepreneurship
    Finance
    Gaming/Casino Management
    Hotel/Motel/Restaurant/Institutional Management
    Human Resources Management
    Insurance and Risk Management
    International Business
    Investments and Securities
    Labor/Industrial Relations
    Management Information Systems
    Management Science
    Music Management
    Operations Research
    Organizational Behavior
    Real Estate
    Small Business Management and Ownership
    Sports Management
    Taxation
    Transportation Management
Business and Office
    Administrative Office Technology
    Court Reporting
    Legal Secretary

Medical Office Management
Medical Transcription
Office Supervision and Management
Marketing and Distribution
    Fashion Merchandising
    Logistics/Operations/Supply Chain Management
    Marketing
    Professional Sales and Sales Management
    Retailing
    Travel and Tourism

Communications

Communications
    Advertising
    Broadcast Journalism
    Communications
    Journalism
    Public Relations
Communications Technologies
    Digital Media Production Technology
    Entertainment Technology
    Photographic Technology
    Sign Language Interpreting
    Television/Radio/Film Production

Computer and Information Sciences

Computer Science
Computer Technology
Information Science and Management/Systems

Education

Education Administration, Evaluation, and Research

Community College Education
Administration
Curriculum and Instruction
Education Administration and
Supervision
Higher Education Administration
International and Comparative
Education
Student Personnel Services
Psychology and Counseling
Educational Psychology
School Counseling
School Psychology
Special Education
Bilingual Education
Education of the Deaf and
Hearing Impaired
Education of the Emotionally
Impaired/Behaviorally Disordered
Education of the Gifted and talented
Education of the Mentally
Handicapped
Education of the Physically
Handicapped
Education of the Visually Handicapped
Special Education, General
Specific Learning Disabilities
Teacher Education, General Programs
Adult Education
Early Childhood Education
Elementary Education
Middle School Education
Teacher Education, Secondary/
Specific Subject Areas
Agricultural and Extension Education

Art Education
Business Education
English Education
Family and Consumer Science
Education
Foreign Languages Education
Health Education
Mathematics Education
Music Education
Physical Education
Reading Education
Science Education
Social Studies Education
Teaching English as a Second
Language
Technology Education

Engineering

Engineering and Technology
Aerospace, Aeronautical, and
Astronautical Engineering
Agricultural Engineering
Bioengineering and Biomedical
Engineering
Ceramic Engineering
Chemical Engineering
Civil Engineering
Computer Engineering
Electrical/Electronic/Communications Engineering
Engineering Mechanics
Engineering Physics
Engineering Science Environmental Engineering
Food Engineering
Geological/Geophysical Engineering
Industrial Engineering
Materials Engineering
Mechanical Engineering

Metallurgical Engineering
Naval Architecture and Marine
   Engineering
Nuclear Engineering
Ocean Engineering
Petroleum Engineering
Polymer Engineering/Science
Software Engineering
Structural Engineering
Systems Engineering
Textile Engineering
*Engineering and Engineering-
Related Technologies*
Aeronautics/Aeronautical Tech-
   nology
Biomedical Electronics/Equip-
   ment Technology/Biomedical
   Engineering Technology
Biotechnology
Civil Engineering Technology
Drafting and Design Technol-
   ogy
Electromechanical Technology
Electronic Technology
Environmental
   Technology/Management
Industrial Technology
Instrumentation Technology
Laser Electro-Optic Technology
Manufacturing Technology
Mechanical Design Technology
Nuclear Technologies
Oceanographic Technology
Quality Control
Surveying and Mapping Sciences
Surveying and Mapping Tech-
   nology
Textile Technology
Water and Wastewater Technol-
   ogy

Family and Consumer Sciences

Family and Community Services
Family Resource Management and
   Consumer Sciences
Food Sciences
Gerontology
Human Development and Family
   Studies
Marriage and Family Counseling
Textiles and Clothing

Foreign Languages

(Includes African, Asiatic,
   Balto-Slavic, Germanic,
   Greek, Indic, Italic, Native
   American, and Semitic Lan-
   guages)

Health

Art Therapy
Audiology/Auditory and Hearing
   Sciences
Cardiovascular Technology
Child Life
Chiropractic Medicine
Communications Disorders
Cytotechnology
Dance/Movement Therapy
Dental Assisting
Dental Hygiene
Dental Laboratory Technology
Dentistry
Diagnostic Medical Sonography
Dietetic Technology
Electroneurodiagnostic (END)
   Technology
Environmental/Occupational
   Health and Safety

Epidemiology
Exercise Physiology/Science
Health Care Administration
Health Information Manage-
    ment
Kinesiology
Medical Assisting
Medical Illustration
Medical Laboratory Technology
Medical Technology
Medicine
Mortuary Science
Music Therapy
Nuclear Medicine Technology
Nursing
Nutrition/Dietetics
Occupational Health and safety
    Technology
Occupational Therapy
Occupational Therapy Assisting
Optometric Technology
Optometry
Orthotic/Prosthetic Assisting
Orthotics/Prosthetics
Osteopathic Medicine
Pharmacy
Physical Therapy
Physical Therapy Assisting
Physician Assisting
Podiatry
Public Health
Radiologic Technology
Recreational Therapy
Rehabilitation Counseling
Respiratory Therapy
Speech-Language Pathology
Sports Medicine
Surgical Technology
Veterinary Technology
Veterinary Medicine

Law

Law
Legal Assisting/Paralegal

Letters

Classical Studies
Comparative Literature
Creative Writing
English, General
Linguistics
Literature (American and British)
Rhetoric
Speech, Debate, and Forensics
Technical and Business Writing/
    Communications

Library, Museum, and Archival Sciences

Archival Studies
Library and Information Science
Library Technology
Museum Studies

Life Sciences

Anatomy
Bacteriology
Biochemistry
Biology
Biomedical Science
Botany
Cellular/Molecular Biology
Conservation Biology
Ecology
Endocrinology
Entomology
Genetics
Marine Biology
Microbiology
Neurosciences
Pathology, Human and Animal

Pharmacology
Physiology
Plant Pathology
Plant Physiology
Toxicology
Zoology

Mathematics

Actuarial Sciences
Applied Mathematics
Biostatistics
Computation Biology/Bioinformatics
Mathematics, General
Pure Mathematics
Statistics

Military Sciences

Aerospace Science/Studies
Military Science
Naval Science

Multi/Interdisciplinary Studies

Conflict/Dispute Analysis/Management/Resolution
Deaf Studies
Decision Science
Folklore and Mythology
Humanities
International Studies
Medieval and Renaissance Studies
Peace Studies
Popular Culture
Sports Studies
Women's Studies

Philosophy, Religion, and Theology

Bible Studies
Church/Religious Music

Missionary Studies
Philosophy
Religion
Religious Education
Theological Professions
Theological Studies

Physical Sciences

Astrophysics
Astronomy
Atmospheric Sciences and Meteorology
Atomic/Molecular Physics
Biophysics
Chemistry
Earth Science
Geochemistry
Geology
Geophysics and Seismology
Inorganic Chemistry
Nuclear Physics
Oceanography
Optics
Organic Chemistry
Paleontology
Pharmaceutical Chemistry
Physical Chemistry
Physics, General
Planetary Sciences

Psychology

Applied Behavioral Analysis
Clinical Psychology
Cognitive Psychology
Community Psychology
Counseling Psychology
Developmental Psychology
Experimental Psychology
Industrial and Organizational Psychology

Personality Psychology
Physiological Psychology
Psychology, General
Psychometrics
Quantitative Psychology
Social Psychology
Sports Psychology

Public Affairs and Protective Services

Protective Services
  Criminal Justice
  Criminal Justice Technology
  Emergency Medical Technology
  Fire Science and Technology
  Fire Service Administration
  Forensic Science/Studies
  Law Enforcement
Public Affairs
  Human Services
  Parks and Recreation Management
  Public Administration
  Social Work

Social Sciences

Anthropology
Archaeology
Criminology
Economics
Geography
History
Political Science and Government
Sociology
Urban Studies

Trade and Industrial

Air Conditioning, Refrigeration,
  and Heating Technologies
Aircraft Mechanics
Automotive Mechanics/Technology

Carpentry
Construction/Management
Culinary Arts
Diesel Engine Mechanics/Technology
Graphic Technology
Welding Technology

Visual and Performing Arts

Art History and Appreciation
Arts Management
Ceramics
Computer/Digital Animation
Conducting
Dance
Dramatic Arts
Drawing
Electronic Game Design and
  Development
Fashion Design
Fiber/Textiles/Weaving
Film Studies
Fine Arts
Glass
Graphic Design
Illustration
Industrial Design
Jazz and Improvisation
Metal/Jewelry
Music, General
Music History and Literature
Music Performance
Music Theory and Composition
Musicology
Painting
Photography
Printmaking
Sculpture
Theatre Design
Video

Appendix II.
Alternate Names
and Related Majors

Aging Studies *see* Gerontology
Astronautical Engineering *see* Aerospace, Aeronautical, and Astronautical Engineering
Astronomy *see also* Planetary Science
Bioinformatics *see* Computational Biology
Black Studies *see* African-American Studies
Business Writing/Communication *see* Technical and Business Writing/Communication
Building Technology *see* Architectural Technology; Construction
Cartography *see* Surveying and Mapping
Casino Management *see* Gaming/Casino Management
Child Development *see* Human Development and Family Studies
Cinematography *see* Film
Clinical Laboratory Technology *see* Medical Laboratory Technology
Clothing *see* Fashion Design; Textiles and Clothing
College Administration *see* Community College Administration, Higher Education Administration, Student Personnel Services
Community Services *see* Family and Consumer Services
Comparative Education *see* International and Comparative Education
Consumer Science Education *see* Family and Consumer Science Education
Consumer Sciences *see* Family Resource Management and Consumer Sciences
Criminalistics *see* Forensic Science/Studies
Debate *see* Speech, Debate, and Forensics
Dietetics *see* Nutrition/Dietetics
Digital Animation *see* Computer/Digital Animation

Dispute Analysis *see* Conflict/Dispute Analysis/Management/Resolution

East European Studies *see* Russian and East European Studies

Economics *see also* Business Economics

Electronics Engineering *see* Electrical, Electronic, and Communications Engineering

English as a Second Language *see* Teaching English as a Second Language

Exceptional Student Education *see* Education of the Deaf and Hearing Impaired, Education of the Emotionally Impaired/Behaviorally Disordered, Education of the Gifted and Talented, Education of the Mentally Handicapped, Education of the Physically Handicapped, Education of the Visually Handicapped, Specific Learning Disabilities

Expressive Therapy *see* Art Therapy; Dance Therapy; Music Therapy

Family Counseling *see* Marriage and Family Counseling

Family Studies *see* Human Development and Family Studies

Farming *see* Agricultural Business and Management; Agricultural Economics; Agricultural Engineering; Agricultural Mechanization/Technology; Agriculture

Fashion Retailing *see* Fashion Merchandising

Financial Services *see* Banking and Financial Services

Funeral Services *see* Mortuary Science

Game Design and Development *see* Electronic Game Design and Development

Geophysical Engineering *see* Geological/Geophysical Engineering

Government *see* Political Science and Government

Guidance Counseling *see* School Counseling

Hearing Science *see* Audiology/Auditory and Hearing Science

Heating Technology *see* Air Conditioning, Refrigeration, and Heating Technology

Hispanic Studies *see* Latin-American Studies

Home Economics *see* Family Resource Management and Consumer Sciences

Horse Science *see* Equine Science

Hospital Administration *see* Health Care Administration

Hospitality Management *see* Hotel/Motel/Restaurant/Institutional Management

Indian Studies *see* American Indian Studies

Industrial Relations *see* Labor/Industrial Relations

Information Science *see* Library and Information Science

Interpreting for the Hearing Impaired *see* Sign Language Interpreting

Jewelry *see* Metal/Jewelry

Judaic Studies *see* Jewish Studies
Language Pathology *see* Speech-Language Pathology
Learning Disabilities *see* Specific Learning Disabilities
Mapping Sciences *see* Surveying and Mapping Sciences/Technology
Marine Engineering *see* Naval Architecture and Marine Engineering
Mass Media *see* Advertising, Broadcast Journalism, Communications, Journalism, Public Relations
Mechanics *see* Agricultural Mechanics, Aircraft Mechanics, Air Conditioning, Refrigeration and Heating Technology, Automotive Mechanics, Biomedical Equipment Technology, Computer Technology, Diesel Engine Mechanics
Medical Records *see* Health Information Technology
Medicine *see also* Osteopathic Medicine
Meteorology *see* Atmospheric Sciences and Meteorology
Ministerial Studies *see* Theological Professions
Molecular Biology *see* Cellular/Molecular Biology
Molecular Physics *see* Atomic/Molecular Physics
Motel Management *see* Hotel/Motel/Restaurant/Institutional Management
Movement Therapy *see* Dance/Movement Therapy
Multilingual/Multicultural Education *see* Bilingual Education
Music Composition *see* Music Theory and Composition
Music Literature *see* Music History and Literature
Museology *see* Museum Studies
Native American Studies *see* American Indian Studies
Occupational Health and Safety *see* Environmental/Occupational Health and Safety
Office Technology *see* Administrative Office Technology; Medical Office Management; Office Supervision and Management
Operating Room Technology *see* Surgical Technology
Operations Management *see* Logistics/Operations/Supply Chain Management
Organizational Psychology *see* Industrial and Organizational Psychology
Paralegal Studies *see* Legal Assisting
Paramedical Science *see* Emergency Medical Technology
Personnel Management *see* Human Resources Management
Planetary Science *see also* Astronomy
Prosthetics *see* Orthotics/Prosthetics
Psychobiology *see* Physiological Psychology
Pulmonary Therapy *see* Respiratory Therapy
Radio *see* Broadcast Journalism; Television/Film/Radio Production

Recreation *see* Parks and Recreation

Refrigeration Technology *see* Air Conditioning, Heating, and Refrigeration Technology

Regional Planning *see* Urban and Regional Planning

Religious Music *see* Church/Religious Music

Renaissance Studies *see* Medieval and Renaissance Studies

Restaurant Management *see* Hotel, Motel, Restaurant, and Institutional Management

Risk Management *see* Insurance and Risk Management

Sacred Music *see* Church/Religious Music

Safety Technology *see* Environmental/Occupational Health and Safety

Secretarial *see* Administrative Office Technology

Securities *see* Investments and Securities

Seismology *see* Geophysics and Seismology

Special Education *see* Education of the Deaf and Hearing Impaired, Education of the Emotionally Impaired/Behaviorally Disordered, Education of the Gifted and Talented, Education of the Mentally Handicapped, Education of the Physically Handicapped, Education of the Visually Handicapped, Specific Learning Disabilities

Statistics *see also* Business Statistics

Studio Art *see* Drawing; Fiber/Textiles/Weaving; Fine Arts; Glass; Illustration; Painting, Printmaking; Sculpture

Supply Chain Management *see* Logistics/Operations/Supply Chain Management

Television News Broadcast *see* Broadcast Journalism

Textiles *see* Fiber/Textiles/Weaving

Theatre *see* Dramatic Arts

Tourism *see* Travel and Tourism

Vocational Rehabilitation Counseling *see* Rehabilitation Counseling

Wastewater Technology *see* Water and Wastewater Technology

Weather Science *see* Atmospheric Sciences and Meteorology

Weaving *see* Fiber/Textiles/Weaving

Appendix III. Occupations Cross-Referenced to Majors

Accountant *see under* Accounting

Account Executive *see under* Marketing; Professional Sales and Sales Management

Actor *see under* Dramatic Arts

Actuary *see under* Actuarial Sciences

Administrative Assistant *see under* Administrative Office Technology

Adult Educator *see under* Adult Education

Advertising Account Executive *see under* Advertising; Business Administration and Management, Professional Sales and Management

Aeronautical Maintenance Technician *see under* Aircraft Mechanics

Aeronautical Technologist *see under* Aeronautics/Aeronautical Technology

Aeronautical/Aerospace Engineer *see under* Aerospace, Aeronautical, and Astronautical Engineering

African American Program Director *see under African American Studies*

Agent, Musical *see under* Music Management

Agricultural and Extension Teacher *see under* Agricultural and Extension Education

Agricultural Economist *see under* Agricultural Economics

Agricultural Equipment Mechanic *see under* Agricultural Mechanization/Technology

Agricultural Engineer *see under* Agricultural Engineering

Agricultural Inspector *see under* Agricultural Business and Management/Agribusiness, Agriculture, Agronomy, Food Sciences

Agricultural Manager *see under* Agricultural Business and Management/Agribusiness, Agriculture, Dairy, Poultry, Range Management, Fishing and Fisheries

Agronomist *see under* Agronomy

Air Conditioning Technician *see under* Air Conditioning, Refrigeration, and Heating Technologies

Air Force Officer *see under* Aerospace Science/Studies
Aircraft Mechanic *see under* Aircraft Mechanics
Airport/Airline Manager *see under* Aviation Management; Transportation
  Management
Analyst *see under* Decision Science
Animal Breeder *see under* Animal Sciences
Animal Technician *see under* Animal Sciences; Veterinary Technology;
  Zoology
Animator *see under* Computer/Digital Animation
Anthropologist *see under* Anthropology
Arbitrator *see under* Conflict/Dispute Analysis/Management/Resolution
Antiques Dealer *see under* Archaeology
Archaeologist *see under* Archaeology
Architect *see under* Architecture
Architectural Technician *see under* Architectural Technology
Archivist *see under* Archival Studies
Army Officer *see under* Military Science
Art Teacher *see under* Adult Education
Art Therapist *see under* Art Therapy
Artist *see under* Ceramics; Computer/Digital Animation; Drawing;
  Fiber/Textiles/Weaving; Fine Arts; Glass; Graphic Design; Illustration;
  Metal/Jewelry; Painting; Printmaking; Sculpture; Video
Arts Manager *see under* Arts Management
Astronaut *see under* Aerospace, Aeronautical, and Astronautical Engineer-
  ing; Astrophysics; Planetary Sciences
Astronautical Engineer *see under* Aerospace, Aeronautical, and Astronauti-
  cal Engineering
Astronomer *see under* Astronomy
Astrophysicist *see under* Astrophysics
Atomic/Molecular Physicist *see under* Atomic/Molecular Physics
Attorney *see under* Law
Audiologist *see under* Audiology/Auditory and Hearing Sciences
Automotive Designer *see under* Mechanical Engineering
Automotive Mechanics *see under* Automotive Mechanics/Technology
Bacteriologist *see under* Bacteriology
Banker *see under* Banking and Financial Services; Finance
Behavior Analyst *see under* Applied Behavior Analysis
Bilingual Education *see under* Bilingual Education
Biochemist *see under* Biochemistry
Biologist *see under* Biology; Anatomy; Bacteriology; Biochemistry;

Biomedical Science; Botany; Cellular/Molecular Biology; Conservation Biology; Ecology; Endocrinology; Entomology; Genetics; Marine Biology; Microbiology; Neurosciences; Pathology; Pharmacology; Physiology; Plant Pathology; Plant Physiology; Toxicology; Zoology

Bioengineer/Biomedical Engineer *see under* Bioengineering and Biomedical Engineering

Biomedical Equipment/Engineering Technician *see under* Biomedical Electronics/Equipment Technology/Biomedical Engineering Technology

Biomedical Researcher *see* Biomedical Science

Biostatistician *see under* Biostatistics

Biotechnologist *see under* Biotechnology

Boat Designer *see under* Naval Architecture and Marine Engineering

Book Dealer *see under Literature*

Botanist *see* Botany

Broadcast Journalist *see under* Broadcast Journalism

Building Inspector *see under* Construction/Management

Business Analyst *see under* Operations Research

Business Manager *see under* Business Management and Administration; Small Business Management and Ownership; International Business; Decision Science

Business Planner *see under* Management Science

Business Teacher *see under* Business Education

Buyer *see under* Fashion Merchandising; Logistics/Operations/Supply Chain Management

Cardiovascular Technologist *see under* Cardiovascular Technology

Career Counselor *see under* Counseling Psychology; Human Resources Management; School Counseling; Student Personnel Services

Carpenter *see under* Carpentry

Cartographer *see under* Surveying and Mapping Sciences/Technology; Geography

Casino Manager *see under* Gaming/Casino Management

Cellular/Molecular Biologist *see under* Cellular/Molecular Biology

Ceramic Engineer *see under* Ceramics Engineering

Ceramics Artist *see under* Ceramics

Chef *see under* Culinary Arts

Chemical Engineer *see under* Chemical Engineering

Chemist *see under* Chemistry; Geochemistry; Inorganic Chemistry; Organic Chemistry; Physical Chemistry; Pharmaceutical Chemistry

Child Life Specialist *see under* Child Life

Chiropractor *see under* Chiropractic Medicine

Choir Director *see under* Church/Religious Music; Music, General

Choreographer *see under* Dance

City/Community Planner *see under* Urban and Regional Planning

Civil Engineer *see under* Civil Engineering

Civil Engineering Technician *see under* Civil Engineering Technology

Clothing/Fabric Designer *see under* Fashion Design; Textiles and Clothing; Fiber/Textiles/Weaving

Coach, Athletic *see under* Physical Education; Sports Psychology, Exercise Physiology; Kinesiology

Collective Bargainer *see under* Labor/Industrial Relations

College Student Services Worker *see under* Student Personnel Services

Commercial Artist *see under* Graphic Design; Illustration

Commodities/Futures Trader *see under* Investments and Securities; Economics; International Business

Communications Engineer *see under* Electrical/Electronics/Communications Engineering

Community College Administrator *see under* Community College Education Administration

Composer *see under* Music Theory and Composition

Computer/Digital Animator *see under* Computer/Digital Animation

Computer Engineer *see under* Computer Engineering

Computer Programmer *see under* Computer Science

Computer Service Technician *see under* Computer Technology; Electronic Technology

Conservationist *see under* Ecology; Conservation Biology

Construction Supervisor *see under* Construction/Management

Consumer Educator *see under* Family and Consumer Education

Consumer Resource Management *see under* Family Resource Management and Consumer Sciences

Copywriter *see under* Advertising; Communications; Rhetoric; Technical and Business Writing/Communications

Corporate Trainer *see under* Human Resources Management; Adult Education

Corrections Administration *see under* Criminal Justice

Corrections Officer *see under* Criminal Justice Technology; Law Enforcement

Costume Designer *see under* Fashion Design; Theatre Design

Counselor *see under* Counseling Psychology; Human Services; Social Work; Rehabilitation Counseling; School Counseling ; Marriage and Family Counseling; Family and Community Services

Court Reporter *see under* Court Reporting

Credit Counselor *see under* Family Resource Management and Consumer Sciences

Curriculum Specialist *see under* Curriculum and Instruction

Cytotechnologist *see under* Cytotechnology

Dance Therapist *see under* Dance/Movement Therapy

Dancer *see under* Dance

Dental Assistant *see under* Dental Assisting

Dental Hygienist *see under* Dental Hygiene

Dental Lab Technician *see under* Dental Lab Technology

Dentist *see under* Dentistry

Diesel Engine Mechanic *see under* Diesel Engine Mechanics/Technology

Dietetic Technician *see under* Dietetic Technology

Dietitian *see under* Nutrition/Dietetics

Digital Media Designer/Producer/Manager *see under* Digital Media Production Technology

Diplomat *see under* International Studies; Political Science and Government; Foreign Languages; African Studies; Asian Studies; Latin American Studies; Middle Eastern Studies; Russian and Eastern European Studies

Drafter *see under* Drafting and Design Technology

Drug Educator *see under* Health Education

Early Childhood Educator *see under* Early Childhood Education

EEG Technician *see under* Electroneurodiagnostic (END) Technology

Ecologist *see under* Ecology; Conservation Biology

Economist *see under* Economics; Agricultural Economics

Editor *see under* English; Journalism; Technical and Business Writing/ Communications

Education Administrator *see under* Community College Education Administration; Curriculum and Instruction; Education Administration and Supervision; Higher Education Administration; International and Comparative Education; Student Personnel Services

Educational Analyst *see under* International and Comparative Education

Electrical Engineer *see under* Electrical/Electronics/Communications Engineering

Electromechanical Technician *see under* Electromechanical Technology

Electroneurodiagnostic Technologist *see under* Electroneurodiagnostic (END) Technology

Electronic Game Designer/Developer *see under* Electronic Game Design and Development

Electronics Engineer *see under* Electrical/Electronics/Communications Engineering

Electronics Technician *see under* Electronics Technology

Embalmer *see under* Mortuary Science

Emergency Medical Technician *see under* Emergency Medical Technology

Employee Assistance Counseling *see under* Rehabilitation Counseling; Marriage and Family Counseling; Social Work

Employee Benefits Manager *see under* Human Resources Management

Endocrinologist *see under* Endocrinologist

Energy Consultant *see under* Environmental Engineering; Earth Science; Geochemistry; Geology; Geophysics and Seismology

Engineer *see under* Aerospace, Aeronautical, and Astronautical Engineering; Agricultural Engineering; Bioengineering and Biomedical Engineering; Ceramic Engineering; Chemical Engineering; Civil Engineering; Computer Engineering; Electrical/Electronic/Communications Engineering; Engineering Mechanics; Engineering Physics; Engineering Science; Environmental Engineering; Food Engineering; Geological/Geophysical Engineering; Industrial Engineering; Materials Engineering; Mechanical Engineering; Metallurgical Engineering; Naval Architecture and Marine Engineering; Nuclear Engineering; Ocean Engineering; Petroleum Engineering; Polymer Engineering/Science; Software Engineering; Structural Engineering; Systems Engineering; Textile Engineering

Engineering Technician *see under* Aeronautics/Aeronautical Technology; Biomedical Electronics/Equipment Technology/Biomedical Engineering Technology; Biotechnology; Civil Engineering Technology; Drafting and Design Technology; Electromechanical Technology; Electronic Technology; Environmental Technology/Management; Industrial Technology; Instrumentation Technology; Laser Electro-Optic Technology; Manufacturing Technology; Mechanical Design Technology; Nuclear Technologies; Oceanographic Technology; Quality Control; Surveying and Mapping Sciences; Surveying and Mapping Technology; Textile Technology; Water and Wastewater Technology

English Teacher *see under* English Education

English as a Second Language Teacher *see under* Teaching English as a Second Language

Entomologist *see under* Entomology

Entrepreneur *see under* Entrepreneurship

Environmental Designer *see under* Environmental Design

Environmental Educator *see under* Conservation Biology: Ecology

Environmental Engineer *see under* Environmental Engineering

Environmental Inspector *see under* Environmental/Occupational Health and Safety

Environmental Technician/Manager *see under* Environmental Technology/ Management

Epidemiologist *see under* Epidemiology; Public Health

Equestrian Teacher *see under* Equestrian Studies

Exercise Physiologist *see under* Exercise Physiology

Extension Agent *see under* Agricultural and Extension Education

Family and Consumer Science Educator *see under* Family and Consumer Science Education

Farm Manager *see under* Agriculture; Agriculture Business and Management/ Agri-Business; Dairy

Fashion Designer *see under* Fashion Design: Fiber/Textiles/Weaving

Fashion Merchandiser *see under* Fashion Merchandising

Film Animator *see under* Computer/Digital Animation

Film Director/Producer *see under* Film Studies; Television/Radio/Film Production

Film Critic/Librarian *see under* Film Studies

Financial Analyst/Manager *see under* Finance

Financial Planner *see under* Investments and Securities

Fire Department Administrator *see under* Fire Service Administration

Firefighter *see under* Fire Science and Technology

Fisheries Manager *see under* Fishing and Fisheries

Fitness Instructor *see under* Exercise Physiology

Food Engineer *see under* Food Engineering

Food Technologist *see under* Food Sciences

Foreign Language Teacher *see under* Foreign Language Education

Forensic Scientist/Technician *see under* Forensic Science/Studies

Forest Ranger *see under* Forestry

Funeral Home Director *see under* Mortuary Science

Game Warden *see under* Conservation Biology

Gaming Manager *see under* Gaming/Casino Management

Genetics Counselor/Researcher *see under* Genetics

Geochemist *see under* Geochemistry

Geological/Geophysical Engineer *see under* Geological/Geophysical Engineering

Geologist *see under* Geology

Geophysicist *see under* Geophysics and Seismology

Gerontologist *see under* Gerontology

Glass Artist *see under* Glass
Graphic Arts Technician *see under* Graphic Technology
Graphic Designer *see under* Graphic Design
Greenhouse/Nursery Manager *see under* Horticulture
Guidance Counselor *see under* School Counseling
Health Care Administrator *see under* Health Care Administration
Health Educator *see under* Health Education; Nursing; Public Health
Health Information Technician/Manager *see under* Health Information
    Management
Heating Technician *see under* Air Conditioning, Refrigeration, and Heating
    Technologies
Higher Education Administrator *see under* Higher Education Administra-
    tion
Hispanic/Latino Program Director *see under* Latin-American Studies
Historic Preservation Specialist *see under* Historic Preservation
Horse Breeder/Trainer/Business Manager *see under* equine Science/Business
    Management
Horticulturalist *see under* Horticulture; Horticultural Science
Hospital Administrator *see under* Health Care Administration
Hotel Manager *see under* Hotel/Motel/Restaurant/Institutional Manage-
    ment
Human Resources Manager *see under* Human Resources Management
Human Services Worker *see under* Human Services; Family and Commu-
    nity Services; Human Development and Family Services
Illustrator *see under* Illustration; Drawing
Industrial Designer *see under* Industrial Design
Industrial Engineer *see under* Industrial Engineering
Industrial Technologist *see under* Industrial Technology
Instrument Technician *see under* Instrumentation Technology
Insurance Adjuster/Underwriter *see under* Insurance and Risk Management
Inventory Specialist *see under* Logistics/Operations/Supply Chain Manage-
    ment
Interior Designer *see under* Interior Design
Interpreter, Hearing Impaired *see under* Sign Language Interpreting
Jeweler; Jewelry Craftsperson *see under* Metal/Jewelry
Jewish Program Director *see under* Jewish Studies
Journalist *see under* Journalism
Landscape Architect *see under* Landscape Architecture
Laser Technician *see under* Laser-Electro-Optic Technician
Latin American Program/Services Director *see under* Latin American Studies

Law Enforcement Officer *see under* Law Enforcement; Criminal Justice Technology

Lawyer *see under* Law

Legal Assistant *see under* Legal Assisting/Paralegal

Legal Secretary *see under* Legal Secretary

Leisure Planner *see under* Parks and Recreation Management

Librarian *see under* Library Science

Library Assistant *see under* Library Technology

Light and Sound Technician *see under* Entertainment Technology

Logistics Specialist *see under* Logistics/Operations/Supply Chain Management

Lumber Industry Manager *see under* Forestry Production and Processing

Management Consultant *see under* Business Administration and Management; Operations Research

Manufacturing Technologist *see under* Manufacturing Technology

Mapping Technician/Specialist *see under* Surveying and Mapping Sciences/Technology

Marine Biologist *see under* Marine Biology

Marine Engineer *see under* Naval Architecture and Marine Engineering

Market Researcher/Manager *see under* Marketing

Marketing Manager *see under* Marketing

Marriage and Family Counselor *see under* Marriage and Family Counseling

Materials Engineer *see under* Materials Engineering

Mathematician *see under* Actuarial Sciences; Applied Mathematics; Biostatistics; Computation Biology/Bioinformatics; Mathematics, General; Pure Mathematics; Statistics

Math Teacher *see under* Math Education

Mechanical Design Technician *see under* Mechanical Design Technology

Mechanical Engineer *see under* Mechanical Engineering

Mediator *see under* Conflict/Dispute Analysis/Management/Resolution; Peace Studies

Medical Assistant *see under* Medical Assisting

Medical Illustrator *see under* Medical Illustration

Medical Laboratory Technician *see under* Medical Laboratory Technology

Medical Office Manager *see under* Medical Office Management Technology

Medical Records Manager *see under* Health Information Management

Medical Secretary *see under* Medical Office Management Technology

Medical Technologist *see under* Medical Technology

Medical Transcriber *see under* Medical Transcription

Metallurgical Engineer *see under* Metallurgical Engineering

Meteorologist *see under* Atmospheric Sciences and Meteorology
Microbiologist *see under* Microbiology
Middle School Teacher *see under* Middle School Education
Minister *see under* Theological Professions
Missionary *see under* Missionary Studies
Mortician *see under* Mortuary Science
Movement Therapist *see under* Dance/Movement Therapy
Movie Director/Producer *see under* Film Studies
Museum Curator/Director *see under* Museum Studies
Music Historian/Librarian *see under* Music History and Literature
Music Business Manager/Promoter/Agent *see under* Music Management
Music Teacher *see under* Music Education
Music Therapist *see under* Music Therapy
Musician *see under* Conducting; Jazz and Improvisation; Music, General;
    Music Performance; Music Theory and Composition
Naturalist *see under* Conservation Biology; Ecology
Native American Program Director *see under* American Indian/Native
    American Studies
Naval Architect *see under* Naval Architecture and Marine Engineering
Naval Officer *see under* Naval Science
Negotiator *see under* Conflict/Dispute Analysis/Management/Resolution
Neuroscientist *see under* Neurosciences
Nuclear Engineer *see under* Nuclear Engineering
Nuclear Medical Technologist *see under* Nuclear Medicine Technology
Nuclear Technician *see under* Nuclear Technologies
Nuclear Physics *see under* Nuclear Physics
Nurse *see under* Nursing
Nutritionist *see under* Nutrition/Dietetics
Occupational Health and Safety Technician/Manager *see under* Occupa-
    tional and Health Safety Technology; Environmental/Occupational
    Health and Safety
Occupational Therapist/Assistant *see under* Occupational Therapy/Assisting
Ocean Engineer *see under* Ocean Engineering
Oceanographer *see under* Oceanography
Oceanographic Technician *see under* Oceanographic Technology
Office Manager *see under* Office Supervision and Management
Optometric Technician *see under* Optometric Technology
Optometrist *see under* Optometry
Orthotic Technician *see under* Orthotics/Prosthetics Assisting
Orthotist *see under* Orthotics/Prosthetics

Osteopathic Physician *see under* Osteopathic Medicine
Package/Product Designer *see under* Industrial Design
Painter *see under* Painting
Paralegal *see under* Legal Assisting/Paralegal
Parole/Probation Officer *see under* Criminal Justice; Law Enforcement
Paramedic *see under* Emergency Medical Technology
Park Ranger *see under* Parks and Recreation Management; Conservation
    Biology; Range Management
Parks/Recreation Manager *see under* Parks and Recreation Management
Pathologist *see under* Pathology
Peace Corps Worker *see under* International Studies or Area Studies such as
    African Studies or Asian Studies
Personnel Manager/Recruiter *see under* Human Resources Management
Petroleum Engineer *see under* Petroleum Engineering
Pharmacist *see under* Pharmacy
Pharmacologist *see under* Pharmacology
Photographer *see under* Photography
Photographic Technician *see under* Photographic Technology
Physical Educator *see under* Physical Education
Physical Therapist/Assistant *see under* Physical Therapy/Assisting
Physician *see under* Medicine
Physician Assistant *see under* Physician Assistant
Physicist *see under* Astrophysics; Atomic/Molecular Physics; Biophysics;
    Geophysics and Seismology; Nuclear Physics; General Physics
Planetarium Director *see under* Planetary Sciences; Astronomy
Plant Researcher/Scientist *see under* Plant Pathology; Plant Physiology
Podiatrist *see under* Podiatry
Police Officer/Administrator *see under* Criminal Justice; Law Enforcement
Politician *see under* Political Scientist and Government
Polymer Engineer *see under* Polymer Engineering
Portfolio Manager *see under* Investments and Securities
Priest *see under* Theological Professions
Printmaker *see under* Printmaking
Production Manager *see under* Industrial Technology; Manufacturing
    Technology
Promoter, Music *see under* Music Management
Prosthetist/Assistant *see under* Orthotics/Prosthetics/Assisting
Psychologist *see under* Clinical Psychology; Cognitive Psychology; Com-
    munity Psychology; Counseling Psychology; Developmental Psychology;
    Experimental Psychology; Industrial and Organizational Psychology;

Personality Psychology; Physiological Psychology; Psychology, General; Psychometrics; Quantitative Psychology; Social Psychology; Sports Psychology

Public Administrator *see under* Public Administration

Public Health Specialist *see under* Public Health

Public Relations Specialist *see under* Public Relations

Public Speaker *see under* Speech, Debate, and Forensics; Rhetoric

Publications Director *see under* Technical and Business Writing/Communications; Journalism

Quality Control Specialist *see under* Quality Control

Rabbi *see under* Theological Professions

Radio Broadcaster/Producer *see under* Television/Radio/Film Production; Broadcast Journalism

Radiologic Technologist *see under* Radiology Technology

Real Estate Appraiser/Salesperson/Broker *see under* Real Estate

Reading Teacher *see under* Reading Education

Recreation Worker *see under* Parks and Recreation Management

Recreational Therapist *see under* Recreational Therapy

Refrigeration Technician *see under* Air Conditioning, Refrigeration, and Heating Technologies

Rehabilitation Counselor *see under* Rehabilitation Counseling

Religious Educator *see under* Religious Education; Bible Studies; Religion

Respiratory Therapist *see under* Respiratory Therapy

Restaurant Manager *see under* Hotel/Motel/Restaurant/Institutional Management; Culinary Arts

Safety Instructor/Inspector *see under* Environmental/Occupational Health and Safety

Sales Representative/Manager *see under* Professional Sales and Sales Management; Retailing; Marketing

Sanitarian *see under* Environmental Engineering

Science Teacher *see under* Science Education

Screenwriter *see under* Creative Writing; Film Studies

Securities Broker *see under* Securities and Investments

Seismology *see under* Geophysics and Seismology

Set Designer *see under* Theatre Design

Sign Language Interpreter *see under* Sign Language Interpreting; Deaf Studies

Software Engineer *see under* Software Engineering

Small Business Owner *see under* Small Business Management and Ownership

Social Studies Teacher *see under* Social Studies Education
Social Worker *see under* Social Worker
Sociologist *see under* Sociology
Software Designer *see under* Computer Science; Information Science and Management/Systems
Soil Conservationist/Scientist *see under* Social Sciences
Soil Surveyor *see under* Soil Sciences; Agronomy
Sonographer *see under* Diagnostic Medical Sonography
Special Educator *see under* Education of the Deaf and Hearing Impaired; Education of the Emotionally Impaired/Behaviorally Disordered; Education of the Gifted and Talented; Education of the Mentally Handicapped; Education of the Physically Handicapped; Education of the Emotionally Handicapped; Specific Learning Disabilities
Speech Writer *see under* Speech, Debate, and Forensics; Rhetoric
Sports Commentator/Writer *see under* Sports Studies; Journalism
Sports Manager/Promoter *see under* Sports Management
Sports Medicine Specialist/Trainer *see under* Sports Medicine
Statistician *see under* Statistics; Biostatistics; Business Statistics
Structural Engineer *see under* Structural Engineering
Supply Chain Specialist *see under* Logistics/Operations/Supply Chain Management
Surgical Technician *see under* Surgical Technology
Surveyor *see under* Surveying and Mapping Sciences/Technology
Systems Analyst *see under* Information Sciences and Management/Systems: Management Information Systems
Systems Engineer *see under* Systems Engineering
Tax Consultant *see under* taxation
Teacher *see under* Adult Education; Early Childhood Education; Elementary Education; Middle School Education; Agricultural and Extension Education; Art Education; Business Education; English Education; Family and Consumer Science Education; Foreign Languages Education; Health Education; Mathematics Education; Music Education; Physical Education; Reading Education; Science Education; Social Studies Education; Teaching English as a Second Language Technology Education; Bilingual Education; Education of the Deaf and Hearing Impaired; Education of the Emotionally Impaired/Behaviorally Disordered; Education of the Gifted and Talented; Education of the Mentally Handicapped; Education of the Physically Handicapped; Education of the Visually Handicapped; Special Education, General; Specific Learning Disabilities
Technical Writer *see under* Technical and Business Writing/Communications

Technology Teacher *see under* Technology Education

Television Broadcaster/Producer *see under* Television/Radio/Film Production; Broadcast Journalism

Test Pilot *see under* Aerospace, Aeronautical, and Astronautical Engineering

Textile Artist *see under* Fiber/Textiles/Weaving

Textile Engineer *see under* Textile Engineering

Textile Technician *see under* Textile Technology

Tourism/Travel Manager *see under* Travel and Tourism

Toxicologist *see under* Toxicology

Translator/Interpreter *see under* Foreign Languages

Transportation Manager/Consultant *see under* Transportation Management

Ultrasound Technologist *see under* Diagnostic Medical Sonography

Urban Designer/Planner *see under* Urban Design

Veterinarian *see under* Veterinary Medicine

Veterinary Assistant/Technician *see under* Veterinary Technology

Video Artist/Videographer *see under* Video

Wastewater/Water Technologist *see under* Water and Wastewater Technology

Water Resource Manager *see under* Water Resources

Weaver *see under* Fiber/Textiles/Weaving

Welding Technician *see under* Welding Technology

Wildlife Manager *see under* Wildlife Management

Women's Program Director *see under* Women's Studies

Writer *see under* Creative Writing; Journalism

Zoologist *see under* Zoology